Contents

Robert De Niro and Martin Scorsese on the set of *GoodFellas*

GoodFellas

MARTIN SCORSESE &
NICHOLAS PILEGGI

Based on the book *Wiseguy*
by Nicholas Pileggi

Editorial work
by David Thompson

faber and faber

First published in 1990
by Faber and Faber Limited
3 Queen Square London WCIN 3AU
Reprinted with corrections 1993

Photoset by Parker Typesetting Service Leicester
Printed and bound in Great Britain by
Mackays of Chatham PLC, Chatham, Kent

Martin Scorsese and Nicholas Pileggi are hereby identified
as the authors of this work in accordance with section 77
of the Copyright, Designs and Patents Act 1988.

A CIP record for this book is available from the British Library

ISBN 0-571-20404-X

2 4 6 8 10 9 7 5 3 1

GoodFellas was first shown at the Venice Film Festival, 1990, where it won the award for Best Director.

The cast included:

JIMMY CONWAY	Robert De Niro
HENRY HILL	Ray Liotta
TOMMY DEVITO	Joe Pesci
KAREN HILL	Lorraine Bracco
PAULIE CICERO	Paul Sorvino
FRANKIE CARBONE	Frank Sivero
BILLY BATTS	Frank Vincent
MORRIE KESSLER	Chuck Low
TUDDY CICERO	Frank DiLeo
JANICE ROSSI	Gina Mastrogiacomo
TOMMY'S MOTHER	Catherine Scorsese
VINNIE	Charles Scorsese
YOUNG HENRY	Christopher Serrone

Director	Martin Scorsese
Producer	Irwin Winkler
Screenplay by	Martin Scorsese and Nicholas Pileggi
Executive Producer	Barbara De Fina
Director of Photography	Michael Ballhaus, ASC
Production Designer	Kristi Zea
Film Editor	Thelma Schoonmaker, ACE
Costume Designer	Richard Bruno
Titles by	Saul and Elaine Bass

Filmed on location in Queens, New York, and in New Jersey, spring and summer 1989

A Warner Bros Picture

This screenplay is the final continuity script prepared by Thelma Schoonmaker, ACE.

GoodFellas

This film is based on a true story.

EXT. A FREEWAY. NIGHT

New York, 1970

Henry's car is seen from the rear, moving fast.

INT. HENRY'S CAR. NIGHT

HENRY *is driving.* JIMMY, *in the passenger's seat, and* TOMMY, *in the rear seat, are dozing off. The sleepy humming of the wheels is suddenly interrupted by a thumping sound. They all begin to react.*

HENRY: What the fuck is that? Jimmy?

TOMMY: What's up? What's up?

HENRY: Did I hit something?

TOMMY: What the fuck is that?

HENRY: What is that?

JIMMY: What the fu—

TOMMY: Maybe you got a – maybe you got a flat.

HENRY: Is there a flat?

TOMMY: Oh.

HENRY: Wha – no.

TOMMY: What the fuck? You better pull over and see.

HENRY: Yeah, yeah.

JIMMY: Pull over.

EXT. THE MERRITT PARKWAY. NIGHT

The car pulls off the road on to the grass. HENRY, JIMMY *and* TOMMY, *who is holding a knife, get out of the car.* HENRY *opens the trunk and steps back. In the trunk a body covered in tablecloths is squirming around. The bloody face of* BILLY BATTS *becomes visible, revealing he is still alive.*

BATTS: (*Gasping*) No, no . . . no . . . no, Tommy. No.

TOMMY: He's still alive. You fucking piece of shit. Die, you motherfucker! Die! (TOMMY *stabs him repeatedly.*) Look at me! Look at my fucking eyes!

BATTS: (*Gasping*) No.

3

TOMMY: Die. You fucking prick.

> (JIMMY *fires a round of shots into Batts's body.* HENRY *goes up to shut the trunk. As he does the image freezes and the voice-over begins.*)

HENRY: (*Voice-over*) As far back as I can remember I always wanted to be a gangster.

> (HENRY *as a child looks out of his bedroom window.*)

To me, being a gangster was better than being President of the United States.

EXT. A GRIMY, ONE-STORY CABSTAND ON A RESIDENTIAL STREET. NIGHT

East New York, Brooklyn, 1955

Immaculately dressed hoods, wearing pinky rings and silk shirts, lounge around the cabstand talking and sipping coffee.

HENRY: (*Voice-over*) Even before I first wandered into the cabstand for an after-school job, I knew I wanted to be part of them. It was there that I knew I belonged. To me, it meant being somebody in a neighborhood that was full of nobodies. They weren't like anybody else. I mean, they did whatever they wanted. They double-parked in front of a hydrant and nobody even gave them a ticket. In the summer when they played cards all night, nobody ever called the cops.

> (*A Cadillac pulls up to the cabstand. The car rises slightly as two huge, dapper hoods get out. Greeting are exchanged on the sidewalk.*)

RONNIE: *Bellezza.*[1] How are you doing? Good, good, good. Nice to see you Frankie.

TONY STACKS: You know Danny.

RONNIE: Hey, Dr Dan. How you doing?

DR DAN: Hey, Tony, how are you? You all right?

TONY STACKS: John.

JOHNNY DIO: Hey.

TUDDY: Hey, Tony Stacks. How are you?

---

1 Sicilian for 'Good'.

RONNIE: *Si benedica.*[1]
> (*The two hoods embrace* TUDDY CICERO, *the sloppily dressed, solidly built man who runs the cabstand.*)

HENRY: (*Voice-over*) Tuddy Cicero.

TONY STACKS: *Minghia.*[2] Could this be the Carnarsie Kid? Hello, Tud.

TUDDY: How are you?

TONY STACKS: Good, good. (*They kiss each other.*)

HENRY: (*Voice-over*) Tuddy.

TONY STACKS: *Minghia*, Tuddy.

TUDDY: Yeah, I'll *minghia* you.

HENRY: (*Voice-over*) Tuddy ran the cabstand and the Bella Vista Pizzeria and a few other places for his brother, Paul, who was the boss over everybody in the neighborhood.
> (RONNIE *slips behind* TUDDY *and grabs him around the neck, while* TONY STACKS *starts pretending to punch* TUDDY *in the stomach.*)

RONNIE: Go ahead. Give 'im a beatin'! Give 'im a beatin'! *Maronna mia.*[3]

WISEGUY: Come on. Come on.
> (*Suddenly they notice that* PAUL CICERO, *the boss, is standing in the cabstand's doorway. He is a large, imposing figure.*)

TONY STACKS: Hello, Paulie.

HENRY: (*Voice-over*) Paulie might have moved slow, but it was only because he didn't have to move for anybody.

TONY STACKS: It's your fault.

RONNIE: You started it.

TONY STACKS: You started it! It's your fault.

TUDDY: Hey, Junior. Here.

INT. HENRY'S FAMILY HOUSE. MORNING

Young Henry's family are finishing breakfast. YOUNG HENRY *is playing with a ball in his room. One of his brothers,* MICHAEL, *is in a wheelchair.* HENRY'S DAD, *a construction worker, is sipping coffee.*

---

1 Respectful Sicilian greeting: 'The Lord's blessing on you.'
2 Literally Sicilian for 'prick'.
3 Sicilian for 'Mother of God'.

HENRY'S MOM *is hurrying the children off to school.*

HENRY: (*Voice-over*) At first my parents loved that I found a job across the street from the house. My father, who was Irish, was sent to work at the age of eleven, and he liked that I got myself a job. He always used to say that American kids were spoiled lazy.

HENRY'S MOM: I know we're late, Henry. Whose shoe is that? Sweetheart, you didn't make your bed.

HENRY'S FIRST SISTER: I'm sorry.

HENRY'S MOM: Henry, don't play ball in the house! Come on, come on, come on. Let's go.

YOUNG HENRY: Don't worry.

HENRY'S MOM: I don't know why you don't get up earlier.

YOUNG HENRY: I get up early.

HENRY'S DAD: Good-bye, sweetie. Take your lunch with you.

HENRY'S FIRST SISTER: Do I have to eat my cereal?

HENRY'S DAD: Of course you do.

HENRY'S MOM: Do you have a sweater?

HENRY'S FIRST SISTER: 'Bye, sis.

YOUNG MICHAEL: 'Bye, sis.

HENRY'S SECOND SISTER: 'Bye, sis.

YOUNG MICHAEL: 'Bye sis.

YOUNG HENRY: 'Bye, Dad.

HENRY'S DAD: 'Bye. Take your lunch.

HENRY'S SECOND SISTER: 'Bye, Henry.

YOUNG HENRY: See you. See you, Mikey.

HENRY'S MOM: Here. Did you say good-bye to your brother?

YOUNG MICHAEL: 'Bye, Henry.

YOUNG HENRY: Yes.

HENRY'S MOM: Henry! Watch how you cross. (*She calls out to him from the front door.*) And bring back milk.

EXT. THE STREET SIDE OF THE DOOR. DAY

YOUNG HENRY *goes down the block toward school, but once out of sight of his mother, races across the street to the cabstand.*

HENRY: (*Voice-over*) And my mother was happy after she found out that the Ciceros came from the same part of Sicily as she did. I mean, to my mother, that was the answer to all her prayers.

6

YOUNG HENRY *is running errands for* TUDDY *and his associates.*

HENRY: (*Voice-over*) I was the luckiest kid in the world. I could go anywhere, I could do anything. I knew everybody and everybody knew me.

(YOUNG HENRY *leaps into the air to catch a set of car keys. Though hardly able to see over the dashboard, he jockeys a mobster's Cadillac into the cabstand parking lot.*)

HENRY: (*Voice-over*) Wiseguys would pull up and Tuddy would toss me their keys and let me park their Cadillacs. I mean, here I am, this little kid. I can't even see over the steering wheel, and I'm parking Cadillacs. But it wasn't too long before my parents changed their minds about my job at the cabstand.

(YOUNG HENRY *watches* TUDDY *laughing with two uniformed* COPS *while slipping them whisky bottles.*)

TUDDY: The best.

FIRST COP: Hey, thanks a lot, Tuddy. I appreciate it.

SECOND COP: Thanks, nice.

TUDDY: This is for your mother and sister. Make sure you give them to her.

HENRY: (*Voice-over*) For them, the cabstand was supposed to be a part-time job, but for me, it was definitely full-time. That's all I wanted to do.

TUDDY: Now take care of this guy.

SECOND COP: We'll see you next week, huh?

TUDDY: All right. Stop back. I'm gonna have steaks . . .

HENRY: (*Voice-over*) You see, people like my father could never understand, but I was part of something. And I belonged. I was treated like a grown-up.

TUDDY: All right, look, Henry. Tell him five nineteen. It's a bad number, okay?

HENRY: (*Voice-over*) Every day I was learning to score.

YOUNG HENRY: Five nineteen.

HENRY: (*Voice-over*) A dollar here. A dollar there. I was living in a fantasy.

RONNIE: Tap the Twig.

TONY STACKS: Tap this fucking twig.

7

RONNIE: He's a good horse. He's a mother.
HOOD: Fuck his mother and his father.
RONNIE: Is that right?

INT. THE KITCHEN IN HENRY'S HOUSE

HENRY'S DAD *confronts* YOUNG HENRY.
HENRY'S DAD: So did you have a good day at school today?
YOUNG HENRY: Yeah.
HENRY: (*Voice-over*) And my father was always pissed off.
HENRY'S DAD: You learned a lot?
YOUNG HENRY: Mm-hmm.
HENRY: (*Voice-over*) He was pissed that he made such lousy
    money. He was pissed that my kid brother, Michael, was in a
    wheelchair. He was pissed that there were seven of us living
    in such a tiny house.
HENRY'S DAD: Well, why don't you tell me about it, then?
YOUNG HENRY: Um . . .
HENRY'S DAD: Why don't you tell me about this?
    (YOUNG HENRY *tries to avoid him, but* HENRY'S DAD *waves a
    letter at him.*)
HENRY'S DAD: It's a letter from school. It says you haven't been
    there in months. (*Yelling.*) In months!
HENRY'S MOM: Oh! Don't!
    (HENRY'S DAD *gives* YOUNG HENRY *a smack on the back of his
    head. Despite* HENRY'S MOM's *attempts to stop him, he then
    takes a belt to* YOUNG HENRY.)
HENRY'S DAD: You think you're so smart! You're nothing but a
    bum! You wanna grow up to be a bum?
HENRY'S MOM: (*Screaming*) Please! Don't!
    (YOUNG HENRY *screams in pain. Freeze frame on* HENRY'S
    DAD.)
HENRY: (*Voice-over*) But after a while, he was mostly pissed
    because I hung around the cabstand. He knew what went on
    at that cabstand. And every once in a while I'd have to take a
    beating. But by then, I didn't care. The way I saw it . . .
    everybody takes a beating sometime.
    (*The beating continues.*)
HENRY'S MOM: Don't!

8

INT. A BACKROOM AT THE CABSTAND

YOUNG HENRY *appears with a swollen and beaten face.*
YOUNG HENRY: I can't make any more deliveries.
TUDDY: What do you mean, you can't make any more deliveries?
    You're gonna fuck everything up.
YOUNG HENRY: My dad says he's gonna kill me. Look.
TUDDY: Come on with me.

INT. AUTOMOBILE

TONY STACKS *and* RONNIE *sit with* YOUNG HENRY *watching the
outside of the post office, pointing to the mailmen as they leave.*
TONY STACKS: Is that him there, kid?
YOUNG HENRY: No.
RONNIE: How 'bout him?
YOUNG HENRY: Nope.
RONNIE: Jesus.
YOUNG HENRY: That's the guy.
RONNIE: Get him.
    (*They get out of the car and approach the* MAILMAN.)
TONY STACKS: Excuse me.
MAILMAN: Yeah?
TONY STACKS: Scum bag.
RONNIE: Come here, you piece of shit.
    (*They bundle him into the car.*)
MAILMAN: Hey! Hey! Hey!
RONNIE: Get in here. Get!

INT. A NEIGHBOURHOOD PIZZERIA

TUDDY *stands in front of a pizza oven.* YOUNG HENRY *watches as*
TONY STACKS *and* RONNIE *hold the* MAILMAN *by his tie.*
TUDDY: You know this kid?
MAILMAN: Yeah.
TUDDY: You know where he lives?
MAILMAN: Yeah?
TUDDY: You deliver mail to his house?
MAILMAN: Yeah.

9

TUDDY: Well, from now on, any letter from that school to that kid's house comes directly here. You understand? Another letter from that school goes to that kid's house . . .
(*They push the* MAILMAN's *head into the oven.*)
In the fucking oven you're gonna go head first.
(*Freeze frame.*)

HENRY: (*Voice-over*) That was it. No more letters from truant officers. No more letters from school. In fact, no more letters from anybody. Finally, after a couple of weeks, my mother had to go to the Post Office and complain. How could I go back to school after that and pledge allegiance to the flag and sit through good government bullshit?

EXT. STREET. DAY

TUDDY *and* YOUNG HENRY *run in the rain to Paulie's house.*

HENRY: (*Voice-over*) Paulie hated phones. He wouldn't have one in his house.

TUDDY: Mikey called. You want me to call him back?

PAULIE: Yeah, all right. Make the call. Go ahead.

TUDDY: All right. Come on, Henry.

HENRY: (*Voice-over*) So he used to get all his calls second-hand. Then you'd have to call the people back from an outside phone.
(TUDDY *and* YOUNG HENRY *run for the nearest phone booth.*)

TUDDY: You got a nickel?

YOUNG HENRY: Yeah.

TUDDY: Get him on the phone for me.

YOUNG HENRY: Yeah. Don't get your feet wet.

TUDDY: Ah, don't worry.

HENRY: (*Voice-over*) There were guys, that's all they did all day long, was take care of Paulie's phone calls.

EXT. MOB SOCIAL CLUB. DAY

In a rear yard, HOODS *are cooking sausages and peppers on a grill.*
PAULIE CICERO *holds court, his bulldog at his feet. Only* TUDDY
actually speaks to him directly, whispering in his ear.

DR DAN: He looks like Tuddy.

PAULIE: All right. Hey.

DR DAN: *Te piace 'a sasiccia?*[1]

WISEGUY: *A sasiccia e' bona.*[2]

HENRY: (*Voice-over*) For a guy who moved all day long, Paulie didn't talk to six people. If there was a union problem or, say, a beef in numbers, then only the top guys could meet with Paulie to discuss the problem.

WISEGUY: Ask Paulie if it's all right to do that thing.

HENRY: (*Voice-over*) Everything was one-on-one. Paulie hated conferences. He didn't want anybody hearing what he said, and he didn't want anybody listening to what he was being told.

TUDDY: (*Whispering to* PAULIE) Charlie wants to know if it's okay to do that tonight.

HENRY: (*Voice-over*) Hundreds of guys depended on Paulie and he got a piece of everything they made. It was tribute, just like in the old country, except they were doing it here in America. And all they got from Paulie was protection from other guys looking to rip them off. And that's what it's all about. That's what the FBI could never understand. That what Paulie and the organization does is offer protection for people who can't go to the cops. That's it. That's all it is. They're like the police department for wiseguys.

DR DAN: I hope they don't look like his dog over there. If they're that ugly you can . . .

EXT. A RIVAL CAB STAND. NIGHT

Using a hammer, YOUNG HENRY *breaks the windows of a row of cars, then pours petrol and throws lighted rags into them.*

HENRY: (*Voice-over*) People looked at me differently and they knew I was with somebody. I didn't have to wait in line at the bakery on Sunday mornings anymore for fresh bread. And the owner knew who I was with and he'd come from around the counter. No matter how many people were waiting, I was taken care of first. Our neighbours didn't park

1 Sicilian for 'You like the sausage?'
2 Sicilian for 'The sausage is good.'

11

in our driveway anymore even though we didn't have a car. At thirteen, I was making more money than most of the grown-ups in the neighborhood. I mean, I had more money than I could spend. I had it all.

(*The cars explode. As* YOUNG HENRY *runs away, the frame freezes.*)

HENRY: (*Voice-over*) One day . . . one day some of the kids from the neighbourhood carried my mother's groceries all the way home. You know why? It was out of respect.

EXT. HENRY'S HOUSE. DAY

HENRY'S MOM *opens the door, and sees* YOUNG HENRY *dressed in lizard shoes, silk shirt and tie, and double-breasted jacket.*

YOUNG HENRY: Hi, Mom. What do you think? Look at my shoes. Aren't they great?

HENRY'S MOM: My God! You look like a gangster.

EXT. THE PIZZERIA. DAY

A BLEEDING MAN *staggers towards the pizzeria, clutching his hand.* YOUNG HENRY *watches from inside.*

BLEEDING MAN: They shot me! Help! Help! They shot me! They shot me!

TUDDY: Henry, shut the door. Shut the door.

BLEEDING MAN: Help me! Help me! They shot me.

TUDDY: Shut the door.

HENRY: (*Voice-over*) That was the first time I had ever seen anyone shot.

TUDDY: Jesus! Can't have that in here.

YOUNG HENRY: Don't worry.

(YOUNG HENRY *starts wrapping the* BLEEDING MAN's *hand in his apron. Then he races into the pizzeria for more aprons to cover the hand until an ambulance turns up.*)

TUDDY: Jesus Christ, Henry, I can't . . . I can't have that in this joint. Goddamn it. Come on, Henry, get away from him. Now get out of there.

HENRY: (*Voice-over*) I remember feeling bad about the guy. But I also remember feeling that maybe Tuddy was right. I knew Paulie didn't want anybody dying in the building.

TUDDY: You know, Henry, you're a real jerk. You wasted eight fucking aprons on this guy. I don't know what the hell's wrong with you. I gotta toughen this kid up.

INT. THE CABSTAND. NIGHT

The camera tracks over sandwiches being made and discovers wiseguys playing cards. TUDDY *and* PAULIE *are there, with* YOUNG HENRY *attending to them.*

HENRY: (*Voice-over*) It was a glorious time. And wiseguys were all over the place. It was before Apalachin[1] and before Crazy Joe[2] decided to take on a boss and start a war. It was when I met the world. It was when I first met Jimmy Conway.
(JIMMY CONWAY *walks in the door to warm greetings.*)

HENRY: (*Voice-over*) He couldn't have been more than twenty-eight or twenty-nine at the time, but he was already a legend. Now he'd walk in the door and everybody who worked the room just went wild. He'd give the doorman a hundred just for opening the door. He'd shove hundreds in the pockets of the dealers and all the guys that ran the games. I mean, the bartender got a hundred just for keeping the ice cubes cold.

JIMMY: All right, the Irishman is here to take all you Guineas' money.
(*The card players laugh.*)

PAULIE: You want a drink?

JIMMY: Yeah. Give me a Seven and Seven.

PAULIE: Jimmy, I'd like you to meet the kid Henry.

1 Joseph Barbara's Apalachin home, 150 miles north-west of New York City, was discovered by the police in 1957 to be the meeting place of Mafia leaders in the USA. This event was the first major exposure of the Mafia's pervasive influence throughout the country.
2 'Crazy' Joe Gallo, the hero of Bob Dylan's song 'Joey', rebelled against the domination of his family's boss, and may have been behind Joe Columbo's assassination in 1971.

13

JIMMY: How you doin'? (*He slips a $20 bill in Henry's shirt pocket.*)

YOUNG HENRY: Thank you.

JIMMY: Keep 'em coming.

(*Freeze frame on* JIMMY.)

HENRY: (*Voice-over*) You see, Jimmy was one of the most feared guys in the city. He was first locked up at eleven and he was doing hits for mob bosses when he was sixteen. You see, hits never bothered Jimmy. It was business. But what Jimmy really loved to do . . . what he really loved to do was steal. I mean he actually enjoyed it. Jimmy was the kind of guy who rooted for the bad guys in the movies.

EXT. A TRAILER TRUCK, NEAR IDLEWILD AIRPORT. NIGHT

A trailer truck is stopped in a deserted area. The HIJACKED DRIVER *is led to a car where* JIMMY *is standing.*

JIMMY: Give me your wallet. You might know who we are, but we know who you are, you understand?

HIJACKED DRIVER: Yeah, right.

HENRY: (*Voice-over*) You know, he was one of the city's biggest hijackers of booze, cigarettes, razor blades, shrimp and lobsters. Shrimps and lobsters were best. They went really fast.

(JIMMY *puts a $50 bill in the Hijacked Driver's wallet.*)

HIJACKED DRIVER: Thanks.

HENRY: (*Voice-over*) And almost all of them were gimmies. I mean they just gave it up, no problem. They called him Jimmy the Gent.

EXT. CABSTAND PARKING LOT. DAY

JIMMY *and* TOMMY DEVITO, *a youngster about Henry's age, are moving large cigarette cartons out of a truck into the arms of a* SCHOOL GUARD, *who is struggling under the load.*

JIMMY: Tommy, help the lady.

(YOUNG TOMMY *helps her to pile the cartons into her car, while* YOUNG HENRY *is keeping watch.*)

HENRY: (*Voice-over*) Drivers loved him. They used to tip him off about the really good loads. And of course everybody got a piece.

SCHOOL GUARD: Thanks, Jimmy. I'll be back for the rest later.

JIMMY: Henry, come here. Say hello to Tommy.

YOUNG HENRY: Hi.

YOUNG TOMMY: How ya doin', Hendry?

JIMMY: Youse gonna be working together. Okay?

YOUNG HENRY: All right.

YOUNG TOMMY: Okay. Sounds good.

JIMMY: Right.

    (*A police car pulls up by where they are standing. The* COPS *recognize* JIMMY.)

FIRST COP: Hey, Jimmy, you got anything good?

HENRY: (*Voice-over*) And when the cops, they assigned a whole army to stop Jimmy, what did he do?

    (JIMMY *slips some bills into a cigarette carton and goes over to the Cop's car.*)

JIMMY: How youse doing, Joe Rich?

HENRY: (*Voice-over*) He made 'em partners.

JIMMY: Everything okay?

FIRST COP: Jimmy, I'd complain, but who'd listen?

EXT. A FACTORY GATE. DAY

YOUNG TOMMY *is taking cigarette cartons out of the trunk of a car, while* YOUNG HENRY *is busy selling them to* WORKERS *as they leave the factory.*

FIRST WORKER: Give me one Pall Mall.

YOUNG HENRY: One Pall Mall. There you go. What do you need?

SECOND WORKER: I'll take two Luckys.

YOUNG HENRY: Two Luckys.

YOUNG TOMMY: Here you go, Henry.

YOUNG HENRY: Thanks a lot.

SECOND WORKER: Thanks.

YOUNG HENRY: Two Luckys. What do you need?

THIRD WORKER: One Pall Mall.

YOUNG HENRY: One Pall Mall. Here you go.

(*Two* CITY DETECTIVES *approach* YOUNG HENRY.)

FIRST CITY DETECTIVE: Whoa, whoa, whoa, whoa. What do you think you're doing?

YOUNG HENRY: No, it's all right.

FIRST CITY DETECTIVE: Why, what'd you get permission from your mother?

YOUNG HENRY: How many cartons you need?

FIRST CITY DETECTIVE: What?

SECOND CITY DETECTIVE: Where'd you get those cigarettes?

FIRST CITY DETECTIVE: Get him outta here.

YOUNG HENRY: It's all right.

FIRST CITY DETECTIVE: Get him outta here.

SECOND CITY DETECTIVE: No.

YOUNG HENRY: It's okay.

SECOND CITY DETECTIVE: It's not okay.

YOUNG HENRY: No!

FIRST CITY DETECTIVE: Get him outta here.

YOUNG HENRY: You don't understand.

FIRST CITY DETECTIVE: No, you don't understand. The store's closed.

INT. THE CABSTAND. DAY

YOUNG TOMMY *explains what happened to* TUDDY.
YOUNG TOMMY: Henry got pinched.
TUDDY: Where at?
YOUNG TOMMY: By the factory. For selling cigarettes.

INT. A COURTROOM

YOUNG HENRY *waits in courtroom. When his case is called, a
well-dressed* MOB LAWYER *comes forward and smiles at the* JUDGE,
who smiles back.
COURT CLERK: Henry Hill. The people of the state of New York
    versus Henry Hill. Docket number 704162.
YOUNG HENRY: Yes, sir, that's me.
MOB LAWYER: Henry, come over here. Just stand over there.
    Now stay there.
JUDGE: Counsellor, proceed.

INT. THE COURTROOM. LATER

YOUNG HENRY *walks out of court, and* JIMMY *puts a fatherly arm
round him and tucks a $100 bill into his chest pocket.*
YOUNG HENRY: Hi, Jimmy.
JIMMY: Congratulations, here's your graduation present.
YOUNG HENRY: Present? What for? I got pinched.
JIMMY: Everybody gets pinched. But you did it right. You told
    'em nothing and they got nothing.
YOUNG HENRY: I thought you'd be mad.
JIMMY: Mad? I'm not mad at you. I'm proud of you. You took
    your first pinch like a man . . . and you learned the two
    greatest things in life.
YOUNG HENRY: (*Sniffing*) What?
JIMMY: Look at me. Never rat on your friends . . . and always
    keep your mouth shut.
    (*Out in the corridor, they discover the whole crew from the
    cabstand, who cheer and embrace* YOUNG HENRY.)
TONY STACKS: Hey, here he is! Here he is!
PAULIE: Oh! You broke your cherry!

TONY STACKS: Congratulations, Henry!
   (*Freeze frame on their smiling faces.*)

EXT. THE DINER BY IDLEWILD AIRPORT. DAY

Idlewild Airport 1963

The camera discovers HENRY *and* TOMMY, *now in their twenties, standing against the hood of a car in front of the airport diner.*
HENRY: (*Voice-over*) By the time I grew up, there was thirty
   billion a year in cargo moving through Idlewild Airport and
   believe me, we tried to steal every bit of it. See, you got to
   understand we grew up near the airport. It belonged to
   Paulie. And we had friends and relatives who worked all over
   the place and they would tip us off about what was coming in
   and what was moving out. Now if any of the truckers or
   airlines gave us any trouble, Paulie had his union people

scare them with a strike. It was beautiful.

(*A* TRUCK DRIVER *gets out of his truck with the engine still running and leaves the door open. He nods to* HENRY *and walks casually into the diner.* HENRY *and* TOMMY *get into the truck.*)

TOMMY: Where'd you get that goofy fuck? What's his . . .?

HENRY: (*Chuckles*) You should have seen – you should have seen the last one.

TOMMY: Are you crazy, Henry? (*Laughs.*)

HENRY: (*Voice-over*) It was an even bigger money-maker than numbers and Jimmy was in charge of it all. Whenever we needed money, we'd rob the airport. And to us, it was better than Citibank.

INT. THE DINER

The TRUCK DRIVER *leaves the diner, then rushes back in.*

TRUCK DRIVER: Hey, you got a phone? Come on! Come on! You got a phone?

DINER OWNER: Over there!

TRUCK DRIVER: Two niggers just stole my truck. Can you believe that shit, huh? Can you fucking believe that?

INT. SONNY'S BAMBOO LOUNGE. NIGHT

The camera tracks through a busy night at a club where many sharp businessmen, bookmakers and hoods are drinking and talking. As HENRY *recalls these familiar faces, they acknowledge the camera's point of view.*

HENRY: (*Voice-over*) There was Jimmy and Tommy and me. And there was Anthony Stabile.

STABILE: Hey, how you doin'?

HENRY: (*Voice-over*) Frankie Carbone.

CARBONE: *Eh, che se dice?*[1] *Come si va?*[2] *Ci vediamo.*[3]

HENRY: (*Voice-over*) And then there was Mo Black's brother, Fat Andy.

---

1 Sicilian for 'Hey, what do ya say?'
2 Sicilian for 'How's it going?'
3 Sicilian for 'I'll see you around.'

FAT ANDY: How you doin', buddy?

HENRY: (*Voice-over*) And his guys, Frankie the Wop . . .

FRANKIE THE WOP: You staying out of trouble?

HENRY: (*Voice-over*) Freddie No Nose.

FREDDIE NO NOSE: Hey, pal, how you doin'?

HENRY: (*Voice-over*) And then there was Pete the Killer, who was Sally Balls' brother.

PETE THE KILLER: By the way, I took care of that thing for you.

HENRY: (*Voice-over*) Then you had Nicky Eyes . . .

NICKY EYES: What's up, guy?

HENRY: (*Voice-over*) . . . and Mikey Franzese.

MIKEY: Yeah, I saw that guy. Yeah, I went to see him.

HENRY: (*Voice-over*) And Jimmy Two Times, who got that nickname because he said everything twice like . . .

JIMMY TWO TIMES: I'm gonna go get the papers, get the papers.
(*In a backroom, a rack of fur coats is wheeled in.* HENRY *is busy organizing this latest consignment for the owner of the Bamboo Lounge,* SONNY.)

VINNIE: Watch it, watch it, watch it. Coming through. Hey, out of my way. I got some furs here. Hey, watch it, watch it. Give me a hand. Over here. Give me a hand. Lift that. Lift it. You got it. That's it. Watch the wall. Here. Coming through. Watch it.

HENRY: All right. Coming out, Vinnie. We got coats.

SONNY: What is this, coats? Coats? Henry. I need suits, Henry, not coats.

HENRY: Suits are, uh, coming Thursday.

SONNY: I know, but this is the middle of the fucking summer. What am I gonna do with fur coats?

HENRY: Uh, you don't want furs? I'll take the furs away.

SONNY: No, no, no. Don't take 'em away. I want 'em. You know what we do? We'll hang 'em in . . . we'll hang 'em in the freezer with the meat. How's that?
(*In the Bamboo Lounge,* HENRY, JIMMY, TOMMY *and various hoods and their girlfriends are having a party.*)

HENRY: (*Voice-over*) For us to live any other way was nuts. Uh, to us those goody-good people who worked shitty jobs for bum paychecks and took the subway to work every day, and worried about their bills, were dead. I mean they were suckers. They had no balls. If we wanted something we just took it. If anyone complained twice they got hit so bad, believe me, they never complained again. It was just all routine, and you didn't even think about it.

TOMMY: Hey, Anthony, Anthony. What was the number today? I can't smell this fuckin' number, Jim, what is it?

HENRY: You never get it.

CARBONE: 528. I played for three years. I can never hit that number. *Buttiglia diavolo.*[1] What are you gonna think?

TOMMY: Hey, Frankie, Frankie, Frankie. What the fuck does 528 have to do with 469? (*Laughs.*) It ain't even close. What are you worrying about?

CARBONE: I know what you're sayin', but for three years? When is it gonna come out? *Buttiglia diavolo minghia*, this way, that way . . .

(HENRY *sees* FRENCHY, *an Air France cargo worker, come in the door and goes up to greet him.*)

FRENCHY: Henry.

HENRY: How you doin'?

FRENCHY: A piece of cake. It's all there. Don't worry about the alarms. I just got to find a way to get the key.

HENRY: No problem, right? Let me get Jimmy. (*He waves* JIMMY *over to the bar.*)

FRENCHY: No, no, I'll take care of it. Hey, James. How you doin'?

JIMMY: Good seein' ya.

HENRY: (*Whispering*) Hey! Frenchy. Tell him. Tell him what you were telling me now, French.

FRENCHY: Too good to be true. Big score coming from Air France. I mean, like bags of money like this coming in, okay? From tourists and American servicemen who change their money over into French money, send it back here. (*Frenchy gets very agitated.*)

JIMMY: Shh. Calm down.

FRENCHY: (*Whispering*) Okay. Look, it's beautiful. Wait till you hear.

JIMMY: Shh. Calm down.

1 Sicilian for 'Devil's whore'.

FRENCHY: It's totally, totally untraceable, okay?

HENRY: The only problem is getting the key, but I got something all worked out.

FRENCHY: Yeah, yeah.

HENRY: You know, me and Frenchy. This fuckin' guy's just a citizen – a piece of work.

FRENCHY: Yeah, this guy's a piece of work. Now if I'm right, there could be like a half a mil comin' in, all cash.

JIMMY: Um-hm. Uh-hm. Good.

FRENCHY: Yeah.

HENRY: And he said the best time is probably over a weekend. So maybe Saturday night.

FRENCHY: Oh, yeah. We got the Jewish holiday on Monday.

JIMMY: Hm.

FRENCHY: They won't find out till Tuesday.

JIMMY: Uh–huh.

FRENCHY: Beautiful.

JIMMY: (*Whispering*) What about the security?

FRENCHY: No! Security? (*Chuckles.*)

HENRY: It's him.

FRENCHY: You're looking at it. (*Laughs.*) It's a joke. I'm the midnight to eight man. I'm the commandant. (*Chuckles.*) He just comes in like he's picking up lost baggage with Tommy D.

HENRY: That's my in.

FRENCHY: It's beautiful.

HENRY: Yeah. I don't think it'd be a problem at all.

JIMMY: Good.

FRENCHY: Huh?

JIMMY: Good.

FRENCHY: We're on.

(*At the table, amid much laughter,* TOMMY *is holding court with stories.*)

TOMMY: That's not, what – what's really funny is with the fucking bank job away in Secaucus. I'm in the middle of the fucking weeds laying down. He comes over, he said, 'What are you doing?' I said, 'I'm resting.' 'Here, you're resting?' (*Laughter.*) On the fucking beach at the park. I said I'm resting! I know I'm resting! I'm resting. They pull me in,

22

they start giving me all kinds of questions. You know, this and that. He says, 'Oh, uh, so what are you gonna tell us, tough guy?' I said, 'My usual, Zero. Nothing.' (*Laughter*.) 'Why tell you?' – the fuck. He says, 'No, you're gonna tell me something today, tough guy,' I said, 'All right.' I'll tell you something. Go fuck your mother.' (*Laughter*.) Bing. Pow. Pooh. Bing. You saw the paper, Anthony? My head was up like this. Yeah. So now I'm coming around. You know, I start to come out of it, who do I see in front of me this big prick again. He says, 'Oh, what do you want to tell me now, tough guy?' I said, 'Ming, what are you doing here? I thought I told you to go fuck your mother.' (*Laughter*.) I thought he was gonna shit. Pow. Ping. Pooh. The fuckers. Ming, I wish I was big just once.

HENRY: (*Chuckling*) You're a pisser, you know? Really funny. Really funny.

TOMMY: What do you mean I'm funny?

HENRY: (*Laughs*) It's funny, you know. Y-Y-You're – It's a good story. It's funny. You're a funny guy.

TOMMY: (*Chuckles*) What do you mean, you mean the way I talk? What?

HENRY: It's just, you know, you're – It's – You're just funny. It's . . . It's fun . . . you know, the way you tell the story and everything.

TOMMY: Funny how? I meant, what's funny about it?
(*The atmosphere is becoming intense.*)

STABILE: Hey, Tommy, you know you got it all wrong . . .

TOMMY: (*Interrupting*) Whoa, whoa, whoa, Anthony. He's a big boy. He knows what he said. What'd you say?

STABILE: You're right.

TOMMY: Funny, how?

HENRY: Just . . .

TOMMY: What?

HENRY: Just . . . you know, you're – you're funny. (*Chuckles*.) So?

TOMMY: You mean, let me understand this, 'cause I like . . . you know, maybe it's me, I'm a little fucked up, maybe. But, I'm funny, how? I mean, funny like I'm a clown? I amuse you? I make you laugh. I'm here to fucking amuse you. What do

23

you mean funny? Funny, how? How am I funny?

HENRY: Come on, just . . . you know, how you tell a story. What?

TOMMY: No, no, I don't know. You said it. How do I know? You said I'm funny. How the fuck am I funny? What the fuck is so funny about me? Tell me. Tell me what's so funny.

(*For a moment,* HENRY *is very uncertain what to say.*)

HENRY: Get the fuck outta here, Tommy.

(*Everyone begins laughing again. The tension is diffused.*)

TOMMY: You motherfucker! I almost had him. I almost had him. Ya stuttering prick, ya. Frankie, was he shaking? Huh? I wonder about you sometimes, Henry. You may fold under questioning.

WISEGUY: Jesus Christ.

(SONNY *approaches* TOMMY *with his check.*)

TOMMY: What the fuck is it with you, he's hanging . . . I thought I was getting pinched already. He's hanging on my fucking neck like a vulture. Like impending danger . . . What do you want?

SONNY: (*Indicating the* WAITER *standing nearby*) This guy's worried about – He didn't want to come over and give the check, you know. Says he . . .

TOMMY: What, the waiter?

SONNY: . . . If you could take care of this here.

TOMMY: Yeah, it's no problem. Tell him to put it on my tab. Of course.

SONNY: That's what I wanted to talk to you about. You know, it ain't just this here. It's seven fucking big ones here. Seven fucking Gs you owe me there. Seven thousand dollars. I mean, that ain't peanuts. I don't mean to be out of order or nothing, but I don't –

TOMMY: (*Interrupting*) You don't like to be out of order? Geez, it's good you don't mean to be out of order, Sonny.

SONNY: No disrespect.

TOMMY: You call embarrassing me in front of my friends and all, like calling me a fucking deadbeat.

SONNY: No fucking.

TOMMY: You know, you know, Sonny, you're a real fucking mutt.

SONNY: What? What are you talking about?

TOMMY: You know the money we spent on these fucking –

SONNY: (*Interrupting*) Come on, don't be like that, Tommy.

TOMMY: What do you mean, don't be like that?

SONNY: Come on.

(TOMMY *grabs* SONNY *by his tie and smashes a bottle on his forehead.*)

TOMMY: Do you believe this prick? You think this is funny, huh? He's having . . .

(TOMMY *notices the scared* WAITER *still standing by.*)

What the fuck are you looking at? You fucking . . . You fucking moron, huh? You don't want to bring the check, huh?

(TOMMY *threatens the* WAITER.)

STABILE: Come on, Tommy.

TOMMY: Uh, do you believe this prick? Fucking guy.

(*He looks at* HENRY.)

You're supposed to be doing this stuff, too, you know?

HENRY: You know what, you're a funny guy.

(*Everyone begins laughing again.*)

TOMMY: Oh! That's it, Henry. (*He takes out his gun.*)

HENRY: No, no, no. No, come on, come on, come on.

TOMMY: That's it, Henry. Hey, you want to laugh? This prick last week asked me to christen his kid. (*Laughter.*) Yeah, for seven thousand I charged him.

HENRY: You really are a funny guy.

(*The laughter is now at fever pitch.* TOMMY *leaps at* HENRY.)

INT. THE BACKROOM OF THE CABSTAND. DAY

SONNY, *with a bandage on his head, is sitting facing* PAULIE.
HENRY *is present.*

SONNY: But I'm worried. I mean, I'm hearing all kinds of fucking bad things. I mean, he's treating me like I'm a fucking half a fag or somethin'. I'm gonna wind up a lamaster. I gotta go on the fucking lam in order to get away from this guy? This ain't right, Paulie. I mean, I can't go here. I can't go there –

PAULIE: (*Interrupting*) You think you're the only one? I talk to them a million times. They don't listen.

SONNY: I mean if you tell him, he'll – he'll stop. I mean, what am

25

I gonna . . . I'm gonna wind up being declared an MIA.
They're gonna find me in the back of a car somewhere in the
weeds? Come on. You know this fucking Tommy all your
life. Who knows better than you? This cocksucker's an arch
criminal. I mean, when I leave my house in the morning,
before I get to the car I'm looking over both shoulders. This
is no way to live – you know I'm no fence jumper. I'm
around you all my life. You tell me what I gotta do.
Whatever the fuck I gotta do, I'm gonna do, no?

PAULIE: What could I do? If there was something I could do,
don't you think I would do it? You know me, I would like to
help you out.

HENRY: Sonny, tell him what we talked about.

SONNY: You think it's all right?

HENRY: Yeah, go on.

PAULIE: What?

SONNY: Paulie, you know, look, I – maybe you could come in with
me. You know, take a piece of this fucking joint. It'd be good.

PAULIE: What are you talking about? What do you mean, the
restaurant?

SONNY: Yeah, I mean this is a classy place. I mean, look at the
layout. I mean, you've been in here a million times. You
know what it looks like. I mean, it – Tommy taking over this
fucking joint is like putting a silk hat on a, on a pig. I mean, I
don't mean no disrespect or nothing, Henry, but, uh, that's
the, that's the way it is. I know you're his friend.
(PAULIE sighs.)
I'm begging you, what can I say?

PAULIE: Uh, what am I gonna do? What am I gonna do? What
does he want from me? What does he . . . I don't know what.
I don't know any-nothing about the restaurant business.
Nothing. All I know is how to sit down and order the meal. I
don't know how to make a restaurant.

SONNY: No, uh, not for you. It's just a place to hang. You know,
I mean, the chef is great. You got a . . . the fucking shows are
good. There's a lot of whores coming in there all the time.

PAULIE: I would like to help you out. Look, what – what do you
want from me? What am I gonna do? Tommy's a bad kid.
He's a bad seed. What am I supposed to do, shoot him?

SONNY: Uh, that wouldn't be a bad idea. (SONNY *realizes he has overstepped the mark*.) Oh, I'm sorry I said that. I didn't mean to say that. I – I just mean that he's scaring me. You know, uh, I just, uh, I need help. Paulie, help me, please, you know.

PAULIE: (*Looking at* HENRY) You know anything about this fucking restaurant business?

SONNY: He knows everything about it. I mean, he's in the joint twenty-four hours a day. I mean another, another fucking few – few minutes he could be a stool. That's how – how often he's in here. You understand?

PAULIE: You want me to be your partner?

SONNY: Yeah.

PAULIE: Is that what you're trying to tell me? You want me to be a partner?

SONNY: Yeah. What the fuck do you think I'm talking about? Paulie, please, come on.

PAULIE: It's not even fair. I don't . . .

SONNY: You don't understand, the joint is . . .

PAULIE: All right, you run the joint. Uh, maybe I'll – I'll try to help you, all right?

SONNY: God bless you, Paulie. I appreciate it.

PAULIE: Okay.

SONNY: God bless you. You've always been fair with me.

PAULIE: All right.

EXT. THE BAMBOO LOUNGE. DAY

Trucks with liquor, beer, sides of beef and furniture are being unloaded and delivered into the front door. HENRY *is part of the team.*

HENRY: (*Voice-over*) Now the guy's got Paulie as a partner. Any problems, he goes to Paulie. Trouble with a bill, he can go to Paulie. Trouble with the cops, deliveries, Tommy, he can call Paulie. But now the guy's got to come up with Paulie's money every week. No matter what.

HENRY: Put that pile over there.

HENRY: (*Voice-over*) Business bad? Fuck you, pay me. Oh, you had a fire? Fuck you, pay me. The place got hit by lightning, huh? Fuck you, pay me.

(HENRY *and the others are filling up the lounge with cases of whisky, wine and food.*)

HENRY: Do you mind if I get one of those TVs?

NICKY EYES: No, help yourself.

HENRY: All right.

HENRY: (*Voice-over*) Also, Paulie could do anything. Especially run up bills on the joint's credit. And why not? Nobody's gonna pay for it anyway. And as soon as the deliveries are made in the front door, you move the stuff out the back and sell it at a discount. You take a two hundred dollar case of booze and you sell it for a hundred.

(*Cases of liquor are carried out of the rear door of the lounge and loaded on to trucks.*)

It doesn't matter. It's all profit.

INT. THE BAMBOO LOUNGE

HENRY, JIMMY *and* TOMMY *are standing around a workman's table. A* LAWYER ~~is going over papers with~~ *a nervous* SONNY.

LAWYER: Sign on the bottom.

SONNY: A fucking shame.

HENRY: (*Voice-over*) And then finally, when there's nothing left, when you can't borrow another buck from the bank or buy another case of booze, you bust the joint out. You light a match.

(HENRY *and* TOMMY *stuff rolls of inflammable paper into the ceiling fittings of the lounge.*)

HENRY: You need any help reaching anything?

TOMMY: You look like you're decorating a Christmas tree, you fucking prick. You don't know what you're doing.

EXT. THE CURBSIDE BY THE BAMBOO LOUNGE. NIGHT

HENRY *and* TOMMY *are waiting in Henry's car for the fire to begin.*

TOMMY: She's from the Five Towns.

HENRY: What, who?

TOMMY: Who? The Jew broad, Diane, I was telling you about inside. I've been trying to bang this broad for a fucking month now. The only thing is she won't go out with me alone, you know.

28

HENRY: No.

TOMMY: No what?

HENRY: No.

TOMMY: No what, Henry? Who the fuck asked you anything.

(HENRY *sighs*.)

I didn't even ask you anything. At least wait to hear what I'm gonna say.

HENRY: All right, what?

TOMMY: Okay, what. She don't want to go out with Italians alone. She's prejudiced against Italians. You fuckin' believe that? In this day and age, what the fuck is this world coming to? So, I can't believe this. Prejudiced against – A Jew broad! Prejudiced against Italians. Anyway she won't go out with me alone unless her girlfriend comes with her. So I figure you come along, you'll go out with her girlfriend.

HENRY: See? I knew it. I knew it. I knew it. I knew it.

TOMMY: You knew what? See what? What the fuck is wrong with that?

HENRY: When is this? When?

TOMMY: Tomorrow night?

HENRY: I can't tomorrow night. I gotta meet Tuddy.

TOMMY: You could meet Tuddy. You could fucking come early and then still go.

HENRY: Tommy, Tommy, why do you always do this to me?

TOMMY: Don't give me that fucking Tommy shit. What the fuck I asked you for, Henry? I'm asking you a favour. I do a lot of fucking favours for you, don't I? I'm trying to bang this fucking broad. You want to help me out? It's – It's like a, it's – it's – it's – I don't understand you.

HENRY: What?

TOMMY: What? She's fucking beautiful. Her fucking family, they live in the Five Towns there. You know, these Jew broads got a lot of money. Maybe the family owns the whole fucking block. You're liable to wind up with a big fucking score here, you motherfucker.

HENRY: Oh, fuck! See! You with your fucking mouth!

TOMMY: Me?

(*They suddenly notice smoke coming out of the windows of the Bamboo Lounge, and drive off sharply.*)

At one end of the table are seated TOMMY *and* DIANE, *at the other*
KAREN *and a very distracted* HENRY.

HENRY: (*Voice-over*) I had a meeting with Tuddy around eleven
   o'clock and here I am a backup guy for Tommy.

TOMMY: So how 'bout you, honey? Did you have enough to eat?

DIANE: Yeah, it was delicious.

TOMMY: Yeah.

DIANE: I'm just watching my diet.

TOMMY: You let me watch your figure for you.

HENRY: (*Voice-over*) I couldn't wait to get away. I was ordering
   the dessert when they were eating dinner. When they were
   having coffee I was asking for the check. I had business.

KAREN: Have some coffee, it'll wake you up.

HENRY: Joe, can we have the check?

TOMMY: Oh, oh, oh, what are you doing? What are you doing?

HENRY: I gotta go.

TOMMY: Go where, Henry, we just got here.

HENRY: I got that thing. I gotta go.

TOMMY: Oh, I forgot about it. All right, wait a couple of minutes.
   We'll all leave together, okay? This way you don't go out like
   a bunch of hobos staggering out one at a time, huh?
   (DIANE *laughs.*)
   I was just . . .

KAREN: (*Voice-over*) I couldn't stand him. I thought he was really
   obnoxious. He kept fidgeting around.
   (HENRY *fiddles with his cigarette lighter.*)

KAREN: You don't mind, do you? That's very annoying.

TOMMY: It's, uh, anisette. Good, huh?

DIANE: Hm.

TOMMY: Yeah, you'd probably do a lot better with Manischewitz,
   but it'd look funny on my table. (*Chuckles.*)

HENRY: Ready?

TOMMY: Henry, lighten up. We – We just got here. What are you
   doing? Take it easy.

EXT. THE RESTAURANT PARKING LOT. NIGHT

HENRY *pushes* KAREN *into his car.*

KAREN: (*Voice-over*) Before it was even time to go home he was pushing me into the car and . . .

EXT. KAREN'S HOUSE. NIGHT

HENRY *hurries* KAREN *out of his car.*

KAREN: (*Voice-over*) . . . then pulling me out. It was ridiculous. But Diane and Tommy made us promise to meet them again on Friday night. We agreed. Of course when Friday night came around Henry stood me up.

INT. THE VILLA CAPRA RESTAURANT. NIGHT

TOMMY, DIANE *and* KAREN *are seated as before, but* HENRY *is absent.* KAREN *bursts into tears.*

TOMMY: I feel terrible. I don't know where he is. And you know he really liked you too. I mean, that's all he could do was talk about her, you know.

KAREN: (*Voice-over*) We were a trio instead of a double date that night.

TOMMY: You know he would'a called. It might – I hope it's not too serious. That's what I'm worried about. I'm –

KAREN: (*Voice-over*) But I made Tommy take me looking for him.

EXT. THE CABSTAND. NIGHT

HENRY *and various* HOODS *are standing around the sidewalk when suddenly Tommy's car screeches up beside them.* HENRY *looks scared.*

HOOD: Son-of-a-bitch!

TUDDY: Tommy, what the fuck?

KAREN: (*Charging out of the car at* HENRY) You got some nerve standing me up. Nobody does that to me. Who the hell do you think you are, Frankie Valli or some kind of big shot? (*Laughter breaks out among the* HOODS.)

31

HENRY: Slow down. Slow down, all right, I forgot. I thought it
was next week.
KAREN: It was Friday. It was this Friday, and you agreed, so
you're a liar!
HENRY: Come, come, come on. We can talk about this, all right.
Take it easy.
KAREN: Talk about it? Talk to you after what you just did to me?
Forget it. I'm not talking to you about anything.
HENRY: Now wait a second. I thought you were going to stand
me up. You looked bored. You didn't say anything. What do
you expect. Hmm?
(KAREN *begins to smile a little*.)
Huh? Let me make it up to you? Karen?
KAREN: I'll think about it.
HENRY: (*Voice-over*) I remember, she screaming on the street and
I mean loud, but she looked good.
HENRY: All right?
KAREN: I'll think about it.
HENRY: (*Chuckles*) Come on.
KAREN: (*Laughing*) It's gonna cost you a lot.
HENRY: (*Voice-over*) She had these great eyes. Just like Liz
Taylor's. At least that's what I thought.

INT. THE ENTRANCE TO KAREN'S HOME. EVENING

HENRY *is at the door, smartly dressed with an open-necked shirt
revealing a gold cross on a chain.*
KAREN: Hello, Henry.
HENRY: You ready?
KAREN: Yeah.
HENRY: Come on.
KAREN: (*Seeing the cross*) Oh, no. Wait a minute.
HENRY: What? What?
KAREN: Quick. You have to cover that cross. My mother sees that
cross, my mother's gonna think that –
KAREN'S MOM: (*Interrupting*) Karen?
KAREN: Mom, I'd like you to meet my friend, Henry Hill.
KAREN'S MOM: How do you do?
HENRY: Hi.

KAREN'S MOM: My daughter says that you're half-Jewish?
HENRY: Umm. Just the good half.
    (KAREN'S MOM *laughs*.)

EXT. THE COPACABANA. NIGHT

HENRY *gives his car keys and a $20 bill to a* CAR WATCHER.
CAR WATCHER: Thank you, sir.
HENRY: All right, I'll see you later. Thanks.
KAREN: What are you doing? You're leaving the car?
HENRY: He watches the car for me. It's easier than leaving it at a
    garage and waiting. It's a lot quicker that way. You know
    what I mean? Huh?
    (*Across the street outside the club, a long line of patrons wait to go
    in. Followed in one continuous camera movement,* HENRY *takes*
    KAREN *through a side entrance, passing by the* BOUNCER *and*
    COPA DOORMAN *who know him, and through the kitchens into
    the club itself*.)
HENRY: Excuse me. I like going this way. It's better than waiting
    in line. How you doing?
BOUNCER: Good.
HENRY: Good, good. What's up? Here you go. How you doing,
    Gino?
GINO: Hi, Henry. How are you?
HENRY: Good, good. Hey.
COPA DOORMAN: Hey.
    (*They pass a couple kissing in the corridor*.)
HENRY: Every time I come here. Every time, you two.
    (KAREN *laughs*.)
    Don't you work?
    (*In the kitchens, the* COOKS *are arguing away*.)
COOK: How you doing?
HENRY: Hey! How you doing?
FIRST WAITER: All right.
HENRY: How are you? Whoa.
KAREN: What would I . . .
    (*They arrive in the club*.)
HENRY: Hey. How you doing? How are you? Hello. How you
    doing?

33

COPA CAPTAIN: Henry, nice to see you. Hi. How you doing?

HENRY: How are you?

KAREN: Good, thanks.

HENRY: Great, great, thanks.

(*The* COPA CAPTAIN *orders a table to be carried in for them and positioned near the stage.*)

FEMALE CLUB PATRON: How come we can't get a table?

MALE CLUB PATRON: Hey, how come we can't get a table?

COPA CAPTAIN: Have another drink, fella.

FEMALE CLUB PATRON: Okay.

MALE CLUB PATRON: All right, all right.

HENRY: Tony, thanks a lot. I appreciate it.

(HENRY *and* KAREN *sit down at their newly positioned table, exchanging greetings with a number of patrons.*)

KAREN: You gave them twenty dollars each.

HENRY: It's all right.

COPA CAPTAIN: (*Offering champagne*) Henry, this is with Mister Tony over there . . .

HENRY: Where?

COPA CAPTAIN: Over there.

HENRY: Ahh. Thanks a lot, Tony. Thank you.

MR TONY: *Salut'*. No problem.

KAREN: What do you do?

HENRY: I'm in construction.

KAREN: (*She takes his hands*) They don't feel like you're in construction.

HENRY: Ah, I'm a union delegate.

COPA ANNOUNCER: And now ladies and gentlemen, the Copacabana is proud to present the king of the one-liners, Henny Youngman!

(*As the club patrons applaud,* HENNY YOUNGMAN *takes the stage.*)

HENNY YOUNGMAN: How are you all? I'm proud to be here. Take my wife – please! I take my wife everywhere but she finds her way home. (*Laughter.*) I said, 'Where do you want to go for your anniversary?' She said, 'I want to go somewhere I've never been before.' I said, 'Try the kitchen.' (*Laughter.*) Doctor Wellsler is here. A wonderful doctor. Gave a guy six months to live. Couldn't pay his bill. Gave

34

him another six months. (*Laughter and applause.*) I love this crowd.

EXT. THE AIR FRANCE CARGO AREA AT IDLEWILD AIRPORT

Carrying a suitcase, HENRY *and* TOMMY *are slipped a key by* FRENCHY *and go into a door marked 'Restricted Area'. They emerge with the suitcase, close the door and walk past* FRENCHY *without saying a word.*

HENRY: (*Voice-over*) Air France made me. We walked out with four hundred and twenty thousand dollars without using a gun. And we did the right thing. We gave Paulie his tribute.

INT. THE CABSTAND BACKROOM

With the suitcase open on the desk, HENRY *counts out stacks of cash.*

HENRY: Thirty-five, forty, forty-five, fifty, sixty thousand.

JIMMY: It's gonna be a good summer.

(*Everyone is laughing.*)

PAULIE: Fantastic. I'm proud of you, now. That is a lot of money

for a kid like you, all right? Anybody asks you where you got it, you got it in Vegas playing craps.

HENRY: All right.

PAULIE: All right.

HENRY: Yeah.

PAULIE: Yeah.

EXT. A BEACH CLUB. DAY

HENRY *and* KAREN *have just finished lunch.* HENRY *is trying to pay in cash.*

KAREN: No, no, no. You have to sign for it here.

HENRY: Should I tip him?

(KAREN *shakes her head.*)

BEACH CLUB WAITER: Thank you.

(*Athletic young women and men in white sports clothes walk by. One young man,* BRUCE, *says hello to* KAREN.)

BRUCE: Hi, Karen.

KAREN: Hi.

BRUCE: How you doing?

KAREN: Okay, Bruce. How are you?

BRUCE: I'm okay.

KAREN: Henry, this is Bruce. Bruce, this is Henry.

BRUCE: How you doing? Good to meet you. (*To* KAREN.) I'll see you around later.

HENRY: Do you know him?

KAREN: Yeah. He lives across the street.

HENRY: Oh.

INT. THE COPACABANA. NIGHT

From behind the singer on the stage, HENRY *and* KAREN *are discovered at a luxurious ringside table.* BOBBIE VINTON *is singing 'Roses are Red'.*

KAREN: (*Voice-over*) One night Bobbie Vinton sent us champagne. There was nothing like it. I didn't think there was anything strange in any of this. You know, a twenty-one-year-old kid with such connections.

EXT. HENRY'S CAR. DAWN

HENRY *and* KAREN *sip champagne and kiss in his car*.
KAREN: (*Voice-over*) He was an exciting guy. He was really nice.
He introduced me to everybody. Everybody wanted to be
nice to him. And he knew how to handle it.

INT. MORRIE KESSLER'S QUEENS BOULEVARD WIG AND B-EAUTY SALON. DAY

Morrie's wig commercial is running continuously on a television screen.
MORRIE *himself is promoting his wigs by a swimming pool.*
MORRIE: (*On television*) Don't buy wigs that come off at the
wrong time. Morrie's wigs don't come off. (MORRIE *falls
backwards into the water.*) Even underwater. And remember,
Morrie's wigs are tested against hurricane winds. So forget
about money. You can afford a Morrie wig, priced to fit
every budget. So call me now! (*The address and phone number
appear.*) And come in for a personalized fitting. Don't buy
wigs that come off at the wrong time. Call Morrie's wig shop.
(*An agitated* JIMMY *is watching the television.* MORRIE *is trying
to place bets on the phone while making excuses to* HENRY.)
HENRY: Come on, Morrie, let's go. Jimmy's waiting and you're
past due so –
MORRIE: Henry, you're a good kid. I've been good to you, you've
been good to me. But there's something quite unreasonable
going on here. Jimmy's being an unconscionable ball-breaker.
(HENRY *moans,* MORRIE *returns to his phone conversation.*)
Okay, give him eight to five on Cleveland.
HENRY: Look –
MORRIE: I-I never had to pay the *vigorish*[1] that he demands. Am I
something special? What am I, a schmuck on wheels?
HENRY: Morrie, please! You know Jimmy. You borrowed his
money. Pay him.
MORRIE: I didn't agree to pay three points above the vig. What
am I, fucking nuts?
HENRY: Morrie, what are you gonna do? You gonna fight with
Jimmy Conway?

1 Yiddish for 'outrageously high interest rates'.

37

MORRIE: Come on!

HENRY: He wants his money. Give him his money and let us just get the fuck out of here.

MORRIE: Hey, fuck him! Fuck him in the ear! What are you talking about? Fuck him in the other ear, that son-of-a-bitch! Did I . . .

HENRY: Morrie, will you –

MORRIE: . . . ever bust his balls? Did I? Did I? I could have dropped a dime a million times and I wouldn't have to pay dick! No . . . he's, he's, listen, I –

HENRY: Shh, Morrie, stop, come on, Morrie, Morrie, Morrie, don't Morrie, Morrie, don't, call the cops? You're talking crazy. Stop it now, will you?

(JIMMY *comes up behind* MORRIE *and wraps the telephone extension cord around his neck.*)

JIMMY: You got money for that fucking commercial of yours.

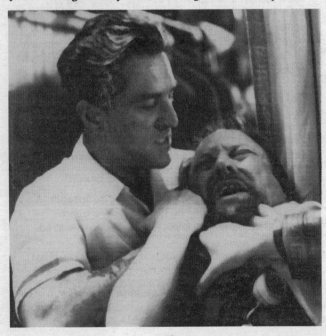

38

Fucking commercial! You don't get my money?! You don't
get my fucking money. Huh?!

HENRY: (*Laughing as Morrie's wig begins to slip*) Jimmy. Jimmy.
He's gonna pay you. Jimmy. Hey.

JIMMY: I'll fucking kill you! Give the money up, you fucking
cocksucker! You hear me?

MORRIE: (*Gasping*) I'm sorry. I'm sorry. Oh . . . shit.

JIMMY: Pay me my money!

MORRIE: I'm sorry, baby, Jimmy.

HENRY: Okay, okay, okay, okay, okay.
(JIMMY *relaxes his grip on the cord. The phone rings, and*
MORRIE *picks up the receiver again.*)

MORRIE: (*Gasping*) Morrie's. Yeah, who's this? He's here.
(*He hands the phone to* HENRY.)
Jimmy, I'm sorry.

JIMMY: Yeah, you should be sorry! Don't fucking do it again and
give me the money! You understand? Give me the fucking
money! You hear me? You hear me? I got to come here and
bust my balls! Give me the fucking money!

MORRIE: No, no. Wait. No. I will. I will. I'll, I'll give you, I'll
give you . You got it, kid. You got it. Believe me.

HENRY: Jimmy, it's all right, Jimmy! (*He talks into the phone.*)
Where – shh. What! Hello. What? Karen, s-s-slow down.
Where? Stay there. Don't move. All right.

JIMMY: Just get the fucking money!

MORRIE: Jimmy, I'll pay you. I'll pay you. I–I'm sorry. I'm
sorry.

JIMMY: What happened?

HENRY: It's Karen, Jimmy. (*He races out of the salon.*)

JIMMY: Yeah, and have the money today. Today!

MORRIE: I'll pay you.

JIMMY: Today!

MORRIE: I promise!

EXT. A ROADSIDE TELEPHONE BOOTH ON HIGHWAY. DAY

KAREN *is waiting at the booth as* HENRY *draws up in his car. She gets
in.*

HENRY: What happened? Are you all right?

KAREN: (*Bruised and crying*) Yeah, I'm okay.

HENRY: Well, now, who did it? Who did what?

KAREN: This guy, who lives across the street from me that I've known all my life.

HENRY: What the fuck did he do? Wha–Wha–What he–What did he–What did–what did he do?

KAREN: Look. He started to touch me. He started to grab me. I told him to stop. He didn't stop. I hit him back. And then he got really angry. He pushed me out of the car! (*They drive off.*)

EXT. KAREN'S PARENTS' HOUSE

HENRY *and* KAREN *drive up to the house. Across the street* BRUCE *and his* BROTHERS *are standing around his new car.*

HENRY: You sure you're all right? Huh?

KAREN: Yeah.

HENRY: Why don't you go inside and get yourself together. Go clean up.

(HENRY, *after shoving his gun inside his belt, storms across the street to confront* BRUCE.)

BRUCE: What do you want, fucko? You want something, huh?

(*Without warning,* HENRY *grabs* BRUCE *by the hair with one hand and smashes the gun against his face with the other.* BRUCE *falls to the ground, but* HENRY *continues to pound his face with the gun.* BRUCE's BROTHERS *back off in horror.*)

BRUCE: Ohh! Ahh! Shit! Ohh! Fuck! Ohh!

BRUCE'S BROTHERS: Hey! What are you doing? What, are you crazy? Oh, my God.

HENRY: I swear on my fucking mother, if you touch her again you're dead!

BRUCE: (*Grunts*) Shit! Ohh! Ahh! Fuck! Ahh!

(HENRY *points his gun at* BRUCE'S BROTHERS)

BRUCE'S BROTHER: Don't shoot.

(HENRY *returns to* KAREN, *who is standing transfixed by the door. He hands her the gun, which is now covered in blood.*)

HENRY: Here, hide this. (*Panting.*) Are you all right? Are you all right?

KAREN: Yeah. Yeah.

HENRY: Huh?

KAREN: Yeah.

KAREN: (*Voice-over*) I know there are women, like my best friends who would have gotten out of there the minute their boyfriend gave them a gun to hide. But I didn't. I got to admit the truth. It turned me on.

(KAREN *hides the gun in the milk box at her feet.*)

INT. KAREN'S PARENTS' HOUSE. DAY

HENRY'*s heel comes down on a wine glass wrapped in a white linen napkin. He and* KAREN *are being married in a small Jewish living-room wedding.*

RABBI: *Mazel tov.*

FAMILY AND FRIENDS: *Mazel tov.* (*Cheers and applause.*)

KAREN: Happy?

INT. THE CHATEAU BLEU CATERING HALL

The wedding party is in full swing. Present are PAULIE, TUDDY, MORRIE, TOMMY, JIMMY *and their wives and fiancées, as well as other hoods and friends from the cabstand. Over the loudspeakers is playing the song 'Life is but a Dream'. The camera moves around the guests.*

JIMMY: No problem.

FREDDY NO NOSE: That's good.

JIMMY: Vinnie.

TUDDY: All right. Listen, here's what we do. Johnny . . .

TOMMY: And my mother's gonna get a bottle of Brioschi. It should be –

TOMMY'S MOTHER: Why don't you be like your friend Henry, here. He's got a nice girl. He's settled down now. He's married. Pretty soon he'll have a nice family. And you're still bouncing around from girl to girl.

CARBONE: Hey, Morrie, listen. You know . . . *eo, gi desorde gi degonse.*[1]

CARBONE'S WIFE: Oh, you know what? I meant to tell you . . .

1 Sicilian for 'The money, those things.'

41

(PAULIE *busily introduces his entire family to* KAREN.)

KAREN: (*Voice-over*): It was like he had two families. The first time I was introduced to all of them at once, it was crazy. Paulie and his brothers had lots of sons and nephews.

PAULIE: Paulie. I want you to meet Karen.

KAREN: Thank you.

FIRST PAUL: You're welcome.

KAREN: (*Voice-over*) And almost all of them were named Peter or Paul.

PAULIE: Karen, this is Peter. This is my brother's second cousin.

PETER: Congratulations.

KAREN: Peter. Hi. How are you?

PETER: Hi.

KAREN: (*Voice-over*) It was unbelievable.

PAULIE: I want you to meet Paulie Junior, my nephew.

KAREN: Hi, Paulie.

SECOND PAUL: Congratulations.

KAREN: Glad you came.

PAULIE: And this is Petey.

KAREN: Petey. Hi.

KAREN: (*Voice-over*) There must have been two dozen Peters and Pauls at the wedding.

PAULIE: This is Marie.

KAREN: Hi, Marie.

PAULIE: (*Introducing another woman*) This is Marie.

KAREN: Hi, Marie.

KAREN: (*Voice-over*) Plus, they were all married to girls named Marie.

FIRST MARIE: Hi, how are you?

KAREN: Good, you?

PAULIE: Doesn't she look beautiful?

FIRST MARIE: Nice. She looks Italian.

PAULIE: Yeah, she looks Italian. (*Chuckles.*) Yeah, right!

KAREN: (*Voice-over*) And they all named their daughters Marie.

PAULIE: And this is Marie.

KAREN: Hi, Marie.

SECOND MARIE: Hello! Your dress is so beautiful.

PAULIE: And this is Pete. No. I mean Paulie. I get confused myself.

THIRD PAUL: Congratulations.

KAREN: (*Voice-over*) By the time I finished meeting everybody, I thought I was drunk.

(PAULIE *gives* KAREN *a gift of several $100 bills in an envelope.*)

KAREN: Paulie, you shouldn't have.

PAULIE: *La vita piena di felicitá.*[1]

PAULIE'S WIFE: Welcome to the family, honey. Sunday dinner?

(*Now every wiseguy and his wife have lined up to give her envelopes.*)

TUDDY'S WIFE: So beautiful.

KAREN: Thank you.

TUDDY'S WIFE: I want to cry.

TUDDY: Karen, there's a little something to help you get started.

KAREN: Fine, thanks.

(HENRY *has opened a bag under the table and he stuffs the envelopes into it. As they dance,* KAREN *worries that it may go missing.*)

KAREN: The bag. The bag.

HENRY: What? What bag?

KAREN: The bag, the bag with all the envelopes in it. All the money.

HENRY: (*Laughs*) Don't worry about that. Nobody's gonna steal that here. Okay?

INT. THE LIVING ROOM KAREN'S PARENTS' HOUSE. DAWN

KAREN *is propped up, awake, in the chair. Her* FATHER *is seated on a sofa.* KAREN'S MOM *comes in.*

KAREN'S MOM: He didn't call?

KAREN: He's with his friends.

KAREN'S MOM: What kind of a person doesn't call?

KAREN: Ma, he's a grown-up. He doesn't need to call every five minutes.

KAREN'S MOM: If he was such a grown-up, why doesn't he get you two an apartment?

KAREN: *Oy.* Don't start. Mom, you're the one who wanted us here.

1 Sicilian for 'To a happy life'.

KAREN'S MOM: Listen, you're here a month and sometimes I know he doesn't come home at all. What kind of people are these?

KAREN: Ma, what do you want me to do?

KAREN'S MOM: Do? What can you do? He's not Jewish. Did you know how these people live? Did you know what they were like? Your father never stayed out all night without calling!

KAREN: Stay out? Daddy never went out at all, Ma! Keep out of it! You don't know how I feel!

KAREN'S MOM: Feel? How do you feel now? You don't know where he is! You don't know who he's with!

KAREN: He's with his friends! Dad!

KAREN'S MOM: Will you leave him out of this! He's suffered enough. The man hasn't been able to digest a decent meal in six weeks.

(*They hear a car draw up by the house.* HENRY *walks blearily up to the front door to be confronted by* KAREN *and* KAREN'S MOM.)

KAREN: Henry, you –

KAREN'S MOM: (*Interrupting*) Where were you? Why didn't you call? Where have you been?

KAREN: Mom!

KAREN'S MOM: We were worried to death! A married man does not stay out like this!

KAREN: Mom, shut up!

KAREN'S MOM: Normal people don't act like this!

(HENRY *laughs, turns away, gets back in the car and drives off with* TOMMY.)

TOMMY: What's wrong with you? Henry! You're not normal! She's right!

HENRY: Shut up! Shut up! No.

TOMMY: What's wrong with you, Henry? What kind of person are you? What is the matter with you?

HENRY: (*Laughing*) Tommy. Tommy. Come on. Tommy.

TOMMY: What the fuck kind of people are they?

INT. LIVING ROOM OF JIMMY AND MICKEY'S HOUSE. DAY

44

KAREN *and most of the women who were at the wedding are at a party held by Jimmy's wife,* MICKEY. MICKEY *is busy brushing Angie's hair, while* ROSIE *is attending to Karen's hands.*

KAREN: (*Voice-over*) We weren't married to nine-to-five guys, but the first time I realized how different was when Mickey had a hostess party.

MICKEY: The sheen, the sheen.

ROSIE: Karen, where you from?

KAREN: Lawrence.

ROSIE: Oh, yeah. Lawrence, out on the island. That's nice.

KAREN: Mm-hm.

ROSIE: I'm from Miami. You ever been there?

KAREN: No.

ROSIE: It's okay, but it's like you died and woke up in Jew heaven.

PAULIE'S WIFE: Angie, stop picking at that thing.

ANGIE: It's the one with the hands. I'd like to smack his face.

SUSAN: It's the red-haired guy. He looks like a farmer?

ANGIE: I'm telling you, I can't get through the gate without this guy's hands all over me. So I told him, I said, 'Keep your fucking hands off me, you son-of-a-bitch, or I'll cut 'em off.'

ROSIE: She means it.

ANGIE: I mean, he don't know how lucky he is. I just mention this to Vinnie. I don't want to know about it.

SUSAN: That's the problem. How can you mention it? Vinnie'd kill him. Please.

ANGIE: I don't like to hold this shit inside. Problem is, if I don't, he'll kill the miserable bastard and Vinnie'll be there for life.

MICKEY: You think you got problems? What about Jeannie's kid?

ANGIE: What happened?

MICKEY: He was in an argument. A lousy ten-dollar card game. He pulls out a gun. The gun goes off. Some kid gets killed. When the grandmother hears it and finds out he's in jail, she has a heart attack. She drops dead right on the spot.

(ANGIE *groans.*)

Now Jeannie has a husband and a son in jail and a mother in the funeral parlor.

ROSIE: Ah, come on.

PAULIE'S WIFE: You know, Jeannie drinks.

SUSAN: Well, maybe she's depressed.

PAULIE'S WIFE: Depressed? Give me a break. She's drunk.

CARBONE'S WIFE: Ah, come on. As soon, as soon as something happens you automatically make them out to be saints.

KAREN: (*Voice-over*) They had bad skin and wore too much make-up. I mean, they didn't look very good.

CARBONE'S WIFE: Oh, she's no saint, that's for damn sure.

PAULIE'S WIFE: She hits those kids. It's, it's, it's brutal.

KAREN: (*Voice-over*) They looked beat-up. And the stuff they wore was thrown together and cheap. A lot of pant suits and double knits.

PAULIE'S WIFE: We make our own crosses.

SUSAN: She don't eat no more. She don't eat.

MICKEY: And she doesn't wake up in the morning. She spends her life in a nightgown.

CARBONE'S WIFE: The woman is no angel, believe me.

KAREN: (*Voice-over*) And they talked about how rotten their kids were and about beating them with broom handles and leather belts. But the kids still didn't pay any attention.

MICKEY: I begged her to come. A doctor's note.

ANGIE: The babies!

KAREN: (*Voice-over*) When Henry picked me up I was dizzy.

INT. HENRY AND KAREN'S BEDROOM. NIGHT

HENRY *and* KAREN *prepare to go to bed.*

KAREN: I don't know! I don't know if I could live like that! God forbid, what would happen if you had to go to prison?

HENRY: Karen. (*Laughs.*)

KAREN: Mickey said that Jeannie's husband –

HENRY: (*Interrupting*) You know why Jeannie's husband went to the can? Because of Jeannie! Because he wanted to get away from her, that's why!

(*He kneels in front of* KAREN.)

Come here, let me tell you something. Nobody goes to jail unless they want to. Unless they make themselves get caught. They don't have things organized. I know what I'm

46

doing. Why, I got things organized with these guys. You know who goes to jail? Nigger stick-up man, that's who. And you know why they get caught? Because they fall asleep in the getaway car, Karen. Come on, don't worry so much, sweetie. Come here.

(*They begin to make love.*)

KAREN: (*Voice-over*) After a while, it got to be all normal. None of it seemed like crimes. It was more like Henry was enterprising and that he and the guys were making a few bucks hustling, while the other guys were sitting on their asses waiting for hand-outs. Our husbands weren't brain surgeons. They were blue-collar guys. The only way they could make extra money, real extra money, was to go out and cut a few corners.

INT. A TRUCK ON THE HIGHWAY. NIGHT

HENRY *and* TOMMY, *carrying a gun in a brown paper bag, pull the* TRUCK DRIVER *out.*

TOMMY: Where's the strongbox, you fuckin' varmint?

TRUCK DRIVER: What's going on? I don't know. I don't know.

TOMMY: Easy.

HENRY: Relax.

TOMMY: Okay, don't get nervous! Take him easy! Easy.

HENRY: Come on.

TRUCK DRIVER: Come on, take it easy, Ow!

HENRY: Lower that.

TRUCK DRIVER: All right! All right!

TOMMY: Don't fucking move.

TRUCK DRIVER: Take it easy!

TOMMY: Go ahead.

TRUCK DRIVER: What's goin' on? What's goin' on?

HENRY: Okay, Frankie.

CARBONE: (*Taking the* TRUCK DRIVER *away*) Come on, into the fucking car.

STABILE: Put him in the back there.

TOMMY: Your hat, ya fuck.

CARBONE: Let's go.

STABILE: See you guys at the diner.

TOMMY: I'm riding shotgun.

HENRY: Did you see him give it right over.

TOMMY: Come on, back to the hideout and split up the loot, you
    sidewinder!

(HENRY *drives the truck away, while* TOMMY *leans out of the side
and shoots his gun in the air*.)

TOMMY: Yee ha!

KAREN: (*Voice-over*) We were all so very close. I mean, there were
    never any outsiders around. Absolutely never. And being
    together all the time made everything seem all the more normal.

INT. HENRY'S HOUSE. DAY

Two DETECTIVES *turn up at the house*. KAREN *reacts as if it is a
normal occurrence*.

DETECTIVE SILVESTRI: Hello, Mrs Hill. Police.

DETECTIVE DEACY: I'm Detective Deacy. This is Detective
    Silvestri. We got a search warrant here for the premises.

DETECTIVE SILVESTRI: Would you read it and sign it.

KAREN: Anywhere?

DETECTIVE SILVESTRI: Yeah, anywhere.

DETECTIVE DEACY: It's gonna take a while. We gotta go through
    everything. All right?

(KAREN *nods*.)

DETECTIVE SILVESTRI: Thank you.

KAREN: You boys want some coffee?

DETECTIVE DEACY: Oh, no coffee now. Thanks, anyway.

KAREN: All right. Just be careful.

DETECTIVE DEACY: We'll go about our business, all right?

DETECTIVE SILVESTRI: And I'll take the kitchen.

KAREN: (*Voice-over*) There was always a little harassment. They
    always wanted to talk to Henry about this and that. They'd
    come in with their subpoenas and warrants and make me
    sign. But mostly they were just looking for a handout, a few
    bucks to keep things quiet, no matter what they found.

(KAREN *continues watching television, on which Al Jolson is
performing 'Toot, Toot, Tootsie Goodbye'*.)

KAREN: (*Voice-over*) I always asked them if they wanted coffee.
    Some of the wives, like Mickey Conway, used to curse at

48

them and spit on the floor. (*Laughs.*) She used to spit on her
own floor. That never made any sense to me. It was better to
be polite and call the lawyer.

INT. JIMMY'S HOUSE. NIGHT

*It is Jesse James Conway's ninth birthday party. Jimmy's and
Mickey's guests include* HENRY, KAREN, TUDDY, TOMMY *and
various children. They are all singing 'Happy Birthday to You'.*
KAREN: (*Voice-over*) We always did everything together and we
always were in the same crowd. Anniversaries. Christenings.
We only went to each other's houses.
(*Snapshot montage: various snapshots appear of family scenes,
card games, babies born at maternity hospitals, and drinks by the
pool on island vacations.*)
The women played cards, and when the kids were born,
Mickey and Jimmy were always the first at the hospital. And
when we went to the Islands or Vegas to vacation, we always
went together. No outsiders, ever. It got to be normal. It got
to where I was even proud that I had the kind of husband
who was willing to go out and risk his neck just to get us the
little extras.

INT. HENRY AND KAREN'S BEDROOM. MORNING

HENRY *is undressing by his closet, which holds row after row of neatly
hung suits, jackets and sharp shoes. Round his waist are wedged thick
packets of crisp $50 and $100 bills which he is stacking away.*
KAREN: (*From the other side of the room*) But I got my mom to
watch the babies tomorrow night!
HENRY: Can't do it, Karen!
KAREN: Why not?
HENRY: I just can't do it. I got something lined up.
(*Karen's closet contains rows of dresses, pant suits, blouses, shoes
and fur coats.*)
KAREN: Yeah, but tomorrow night's the only night she can do it.
Pretty please?
HENRY: Karen, I can't do it. What do you want me to do?

49

INT. HENRY AND KAREN'S KITCHEN

HENRY *is now shaved and dressed to go out.*
HENRY: I gotta go.
KAREN: Wait a minute!
HENRY: What?
KAREN: I wanted to go shopping. Can I get some money?
HENRY: How much do you need? How much?
KAREN: (*Holding her thumb and forefinger a few inches apart*) That much.
HENRY: What? (*He takes the amount she wants from his wad.*) Here.
KAREN: This much. (*She puts her hand to his crotch.*)
HENRY: Here.
KAREN: Give me a kiss.
　　(*They kiss.*)
HENRY: Here. See you later.
KAREN: No. (*She goes down his body and unzips his fly.*)
HENRY: (*Chuckles*) Oh, all right.

INT. THE SUITE, A BAR ON QUEENS BOULEVARD. NIGHT

Queens, New York, 11 June 1970

It is after midnight. At one end of the bar, BILLY BATTS *is holding court. He's been in prison for six years and has just been released.*
BATTS: Six guys would appear. They were lined up. I couldn't fucking believe it. It's funny.
VITO: Hey, Batts. Look at you.
BATTS: Vito! Hello. You look terrific.
VITO: Welcome home.
BATTS: How you been? Great. Great. Everything.
VITO: Great. Great.
BATTS: Hiya, sweetheart. How are you?
VITO'S GIRLFRIEND: Hi. Billy. Good, good.
BATTS: Have a seat. Sit down. Have a drink. Come on. Give us a drink. Give them all a drink here. And give those Irish hoodlums a drink down there.
　　(*Further down the bar,* JIMMY *and* HENRY *are drinking with friends.*)
JIMMY: There's only one Irishman here.

HENRY: Yeah.

BATTS: It's a celebration, fellas. *Salut'*.

JIMMY: Top of the morning to you.

BATTS: It's good to be home.

HENRY: Welcome back.

(TOMMY *and a new girlfriend,* LISA, *walk into the bar.*)

JIMMY: Hey.

TOMMY: This is my friend, Jimmy.

JIMMY: Hello. It's nice to meet you.

LISA: Hi. It's nice to meet you.

TOMMY: Henry, it's his joint. This is Lisa.

HENRY: Hi.

LISA: Hi.

HENRY: How are you?

(BATTS *sees* TOMMY, *who is not pleased to encounter the older man again.*)

BATTS: Hey. Tommy. All dressed up.

JIMMY: Would you like a drink or anything?

BATTS: All grown up and doing the town. Look at this.

TOMMY: Ah, shit.

BATTS: Tommy.

TOMMY: (*To* HENRY) I forgot you was having a party here for this mouth.

BATTS: Tommy! Oh! Oh! Tom! Oh! Oh! Come here!

TOMMY: (*Under his breath*) Jesus Christ. Let me go say hello. (*He walks over.*) Hey, Billy, how are you?

BATTS: Tommy, get over here. I haven't seen you in six fucking years.

TOMMY: Hey, Billy – How you doing, Billy?

BATTS: Jesus Christ, almighty. You look terrific.

(*He embraces* TOMMY *hard.*)

TOMMY: Whoa. Whoa.

BATTS: How you feeling, huh?

TOMMY: Watch the suit! Watch the suit! Jesus Christ!

BATTS: Watch the suit! You little prick, ya. I know you all my life.

TOMMY: All right. Good.

BATTS: Don't go getting too big on me, now!

TOMMY: Just don't go busting my balls, Billy, okay?

51

BATTS: Hey, Tommy, if I was gonna break your balls, I'd tell you to go home and get your shine box. (*Turns to his friends.*) Now this kid, this kid was great. They . . . they used to call him Spitshine Tommy. I swear to God. Oh, he'd make your shoes look like fucking mirrors. Excuse my language. He was terrific. He was the best. And he made a lot of money too. *Salut'*, Tommy.

TOMMY: No more shines, Billy.

BATTS: What?

TOMMY: I said, no more shines. Maybe you didn't hear about it. You been away a long time. They didn't go up there and tell ya.

BATTS: Ah.

TOMMY: I don't shine shoes anymore.

BATTS: Relax, will you? For crying out – What's, what's got into you? I'm breaking your balls a little bit, that's all. I'm only kidding with you. Geez.

TOMMY: Sometimes you don't sound like you're kidding. You know, there's a lot of people around, you know.

BATTS: Tommy, I'm only kidding with you. We're having a party. I mean, I just came home. I haven't seen you in a long time and I'm breaking your balls, and you – right away you're getting fucking fresh. I'm sorry. I didn't mean to offend you.

TOMMY: You're right. I'm sorry too. It's okay. No problem.

BATTS: Okay. *Salut'*.

(*Turning his back on* TOMMY.)

Now go home and get your fucking shinebox.

TOMMY: (*Incensed*) Motherfucking mutt! You –

JIMMY: Hey! Tommy! Tommy!

TOMMY: You fucking piece of shit!

HENRY: (*Holding* TOMMY *back*) Come here! Tommy!

BATTS: You little old fuck-face. Yeah, yeah, yeah! Come on! Come on! Come on!

TOMMY: You old fucking fake!

BATTS: Let him go.

TOMMY: Motherfucker! Geez, he bought his fucking button! That fake old tough guy!

HENRY: He's drunk.

52

TOMMY: You bought your fucking button, you fake tough guy!

BATTS: Take it easy. Take it easy. Take it – Don't get nervous. Don't get nervous. Let him come.

TOMMY: You motherfucker. Fuck. Keep that motherfucker here. Keep him here! Keep him here!

BATTS: Come on! Let him – let him go. Let him go.

TOMMY: Come on.

HENRY: Batts! Batts!

BATTS: Come on! You fucking feel strong?

TOMMY: You old fake scumbag!

(*He storms out, taking* LISA *with him.*)

HENRY: Tommy, Tommy. (*To* BATTS.) I'm sorry. Tommy gets a little loaded. He doesn't mean any disrespect.

BATTS: He don't mean any disrespect, Henry? Are you nuts?

HENRY: Not at all.

BATTS: Teach this kid a little fucking manners. Hey, Jimmy, what's right is right. You understand what I'm talking about?

JIMMY: It's all right. It's all right.

HENRY: Maybe –

BATTS: Hey, I mean, the kid's up here. I was, we're hugging and kissing over here and two minutes later he's acting like a fucking jerk.

JIMMY: Well, now, now, now, now, now. You know, you insulted him a little bit. You got a little out of order yourself, I'm sorry.

BATTS: I didn't insult him, I didn't insult him.

JIMMY: You insulted him a little bit.

BATTS: No, I didn't insult nobody. Give us a drink. Come on.

JIMMY: Okay.

HENRY: Come on. Let's have some drinks, all right? Drinks on the house. Come on. Let me . . .

BATTS: Yeah, no, have the drink with me.

HENRY: No, no, no, no, no.

JIMMY: Come on. No, no, no. Billy, Billy.

HENRY: No.

JIMMY: The drinks are on the house.

HENRY: Go on, Fred. Go on. Put it on the house.

INT. THE SUITE. LATER

JIMMY *and* BATTS *are still seated at the bar talking while everyone else has gone.* HENRY *is closing up.*

BATTS: These kids, Jimmy, they got no fucking respect. You understand.

JIMMY: It's changed now these days. You know, you've been away for six years. Everything's different.

BATTS: Yeah.

JIMMY: Totally different.

BATTS: I did my fucking time, Jimmy. I did my fucking time. I came home . . . and I want what I got to get. I got fucking mouths to feed.

JIMMY: You're gonna get it.

BATTS: You understand.

JIMMY: You're gonna get it.

BATTS: Yeah, I'm – What's this?

(TOMMY *returns to the bar unseen by* BATTS *and smashes a gun on the side of his face.*)

TOMMY: You fuck! You fuck!

JIMMY: Get the door!

(HENRY *rushes over to close the front door.* BATTS *is on the ground being brutally kicked by* TOMMY *and* JIMMY.)

TOMMY: Let me shoot him in his big fucking mouth. Let's shoot him. Shit.

(TOMMY *puts his gun in* BATTS*'s mouth.* JIMMY *kicks it away.* BATTS *lies still on the floor, covered in blood.*)

JIMMY: Fucking mutt dented my shoes.

HENRY: His whole crew's gonna be looking for him. This is fucking bad. What are we gonna do with him? We can't just dump him on the street.

(*They begin to wrap* BATTS*'s body in tablecloths.*)

JIMMY: Don't worry. Don't worry. I know a place upstate they'll never find him. Come on. Let's get some more tablecloths.

TOMMY: (*To a shocked* HENRY) I don't want to get blood on your floor.

JIMMY: Henry.

HENRY: Yeah?

JIMMY: Go open your trunk.
HENRY: All right. Got him? Got him?
  (JIMMY *and* TOMMY *pick up the wrapped body.*)
JIMMY: Yeah.
TOMMY: I'll pick up a shovel at my mother's house.

INT. THE KITCHEN IN TOMMY'S MOTHER'S HOUSE. LATER

In the darkness, TOMMY, JIMMY *and* HENRY *enter the house.*
TOMMY: She keeps a shovel lyin' around here somewhere.
JIMMY: Where?
TOMMY: Just keep quiet. I don't want to wake her up.
JIMMY: Yeah, okay.
  (*The light comes on, and* TOMMY'S MOTHER *appears in her housecoat.*)

TOMMY: Oop! Ehh!

JIMMY: Hey.

TOMMY'S MOTHER: Hey, look who's here. Look who's here.

TOMMY: Hey, Ma, what are you doing up?

TOMMY'S MOTHER: What are you doing? (*She sees blood on him.*) What happened? What –

TOMMY: No, no, nothing. I hit, I hit, I hit something on the road.

TOMMY'S MOTHER: What happened to you?

TOMMY: Jimmy will tell you.

TOMMY'S MOTHER: What happened? What happened to him?

JIMMY: Nothing, nothing, nothing, nothing. How are you, sweetheart?

TOMMY'S MOTHER: What happened, boys?

JIMMY: How are you sweetheart?

TOMMY'S MOTHER: Ah, Jim. We haven't seen you in so long! What happened to him? I hate to see him that way. And you too.

HENRY: Hi, how are you?

TOMMY'S MOTHER: How are you?

HENRY: Good.

TOMMY'S MOTHER: But what happened? Tell me what happened.

JIMMY: What are you doing up so late?

TOMMY'S MOTHER: Well, he came in. Youse came in. I figured, you know . . . I'm, I'm so happy to see him.

JIMMY: Do you know what time it is?

TOMMY'S MOTHER: Look, go inside. Make yourselves comfortable. I'll make you something to eat.

JIMMY: No.

HENRY: No. No, no, no, no, no, no.

JIMMY: No, no, no. Go to sleep. Go to sleep. We're gonna leave. We're just getting the shovel, we're gonna change and we're gonna go out.

TOMMY'S MOTHER: No, I can't sleep. Not while he's home. No. I haven't seen him so long.

JIMMY: No, no.

TOMMY'S MOTHER: I want to see him. Go ahead, youse go inside.

JIMMY: No, but you don't want –

HENRY, JIMMY *and* TOMMY *are sitting around the kitchen table*
eating pasta. TOMMY'S MOTHER *is pleased to have their company.*

TOMMY: This stuff is great but it's like lead. Ba boom.

TOMMY'S MOTHER: So tell me, tell me, where have you been? I
haven't seen you. I haven't even – You haven't even called or
anything. Where have you been?

TOMMY: Ma. Mom, I been working nights.

TOMMY'S MOTHER: And?

TOMMY: And, well, tonight we were out late. We took a ride on
the . . . out to the country and we hit one of those deers.
That's where all the blood came from. I told you. Jimmy told
you before. I went to change.

TOMMY'S MOTHER: And?

TOMMY: Anyway, you know, it reminds me, Ma. I need this
knife. I'm gonna take this. It's okay?

TOMMY'S MOTHER: Okay, yeah. Bring it back, though, you
know.

TOMMY: I just need it for a little while. Well the poor thing, you
know, he got – I hit him in his, uh – We hit the deer and his
paw – What do you call it?

TOMMY'S MOTHER: The paw. The paw. His foot.

TOMMY: The paw, uh . . .

JIMMY: The hoof.

TOMMY: The hoof got caught in that grill. I got to, I got to hack it
off.

TOMMY'S MOTHER: Ooh!

TOMMY: M-M-Ma it's a sin. You gonna leave it there, you know?
So anyway, I'll, I'll bring your knife back after . . .
Anyway . . .

JIMMY: Delicious. Delicious.

TOMMY'S MOTHER: Thank you. (*To* TOMMY.) Why don't you
get yourself a nice girl?

TOMMY: I get a nice one almost every night, Ma.

TOMMY'S MOTHER: Yeah, but get yourself a girl so you can settle
down. That's what I mean.

TOMMY: I settle down almost every night, but then in the

morning I'm free. I love you! I wanna be wi– (*He kisses her.*) I
wanna be with you!

TOMMY'S MOTHER: Why?

JIMMY: Why don't you settle down?

TOMMY'S MOTHER: How's your friend, Henry there? Henry,
what's the matter? You don't talk too much.

JIMMY: You should talk a little bit. What are you quiet for?

TOMMY'S MOTHER: He don't eat much. He don't talk much.

HENRY: I-I'm just listening.

TOMMY: What's the matter? Something wrong with you?

HENRY: No.

TOMMY'S MOTHER: You remind me of when we were kids. The
compares used to visit one another. And there was this man.
He would never talk. He would just sit there all night and
not say a word. So, they says to him, 'What's the matter,
compare, don't you talk? Don't you say anything?' He says,
'What am I gonna say, that my wife two-times me?' So, she
says to him, 'Shut up! You're always talking!' (*They all
laugh.*) But in Italian, it sounds much nicer, you know.

TOMMY: *Cornuto content.*

TOMMY'S MOTHER: Yeah. That's it.

JIMMY: What's that mean?

TOMMY: *Cornuto* means he's, he's content to be jerk.

JIMMY: Ah.

TOMMY'S MOTHER: Or he's —

TOMMY: (*Interrupting*) He doesn't care who knows it. He's content.

TOMMY'S MOTHER: Did, uh, did Tommy ever tell you about my
   painting?

JIMMY: No.

TOMMY'S MOTHER: Look at this.

   (*She shows them a small oil painting in a very naïve style of an
   old man and two dogs in a small boat.*)

JIMMY: Ah, it's beautiful.

TOMMY: I like this one. The dog, one dog goes one way and the
   other dog goes the other way. How come?

TOMMY'S MOTHER: One is going east and the other is going west.
   So what?

TOMMY: And this guy's saying, 'What do you want from me?'
   The guy's got a nice head of white hair. Look how beautiful.
   The dog it looks the same.

JIMMY: Looks like somebody we know.

   (JIMMY *and* TOMMY *laugh at the old man's resemblance to*
   BATTS.)

TOMMY: Without the beard. No, it's him! It's him! Ohh . . .

INT. HENRY'S CAR. NIGHT

As in the opening scene, HENRY, JIMMY *and* TOMMY *are startled by
a strange thumping noise.*

HENRY: What the fuck is that? Did I hit something?

HENRY: (*Voice-over*) For most of the guys, killings got to be
   accepted.

TOMMY: What's up? What's up?

HENRY: (*Voice-over*) Murder was the only way that everybody
   stayed in line. You got out of line, you got whacked.
   Everybody knew the rules. But sometimes, even if people
   didn't get out of line, they got whacked. I mean, hits just
   became a habit for some of the guys. Guys would get into

arguments over nothing and before you knew it, one of them was dead. And they were shooting each other all the time. Shooting people was a normal thing. It was no big deal. (*As before,* HENRY *opens the trunk of the car, and* TOMMY *and* JIMMY *finish off the dying* BATTS. *Then they bury him in a Connecticut woodland.*)

HENRY: (*Voice-over*) We had a, we had a serious problem with Billy Batts. This was really a touchy thing. Tommy'd killed a made guy. Batts was part of the Gambino crew and was considered untouchable. And before you could touch a made guy, you had to have good reason. You had to have a sitdown, and you better get an okay, or you'd be the one that got whacked.

INT. THE COPACABANA. NIGHT

HENRY, TOMMY *and other hoods greet their friends.*

FRANKIE: How are you?

COPA CAPTAIN: That's good.

GODFATHER AT TABLE: How's it going, hey?

TOMMY: Good to see you, Vito!

VITO: Hey, how are you, buddy?

HENRY: Hey. How you doing? Good seeing you again.

GODFATHER AT TABLE: Okay, thank you.

HENRY: (*Voice-over*) Saturday night was for wives, but Friday night at the Copa was always for the girlfriends.

CARBONE: *Maronna mia, ste picciote so' veramente bone.*[1]
(HENRY, TOMMY *and* CARBONE *are now entertaining some girls at their table. The girl with* HENRY *is* JANICE ROSSI.)

JANICE: And last week we saw Sammy Davis Junior. You gotta see this show. What a performer. He does these impersonations. I swear you would think it was the real people!

TOMMY'S COPA GIRLFRIEND: Oh, it's unbelievable. I mean, you could see how a white girl could fall for him.

TOMMY: What?

TOMMY'S COPA GIRLFRIEND: Well, I mean, not me. I'm just saying, like, you could see how some girls could. You know,

1 Sicilian for 'Mother of God, these girls are really good.'

like that Swedish girl.

TOMMY: In other words, you condone that stuff.

HENRY: (*Chuckling*) Take it easy.

TOMMY: Oh, Henry . . .

HENRY: I know. I know.

TOMMY: . . . I want to make sure I don't wind up kissing fucking Nat King Cole over here. You know what I talking about?

TOMMY'S COPA GIRLFRIEND: No, I'm not talking about me. I wasn't . . . I'm not talking about me, although you could see how a girl could. You know, he's got personality.

TOMMY: (*Grunts*) Of course. Yeah.

CARBONE: *Minghia, ancora chesta 'cca* with the personality!

TOMMY'S COPA GIRLFRIEND: Yeah.

TOMMY: Yeah. He's very talented. I understand perfectly what you're saying, but you have to watch out sometimes how you say things, you know, people get the wrong impression.

TOMMY'S COPA GIRLFRIEND: I just said he was talented. You know, he's just unbelievable.

TOMMY: Why don't you just leave it alone now? I mean, I understand what you said. The guy's talented. Leave it at that. He's very talented.

TOMMY'S COPA GIRLFRIEND: Okay. Fine.

(*On stage,* JERRY VALE *sings 'Pretend You Don't See Her'.*)

EXT. JANICE'S APARTMENT BUILDING. NIGHT

With the song continuing, HENRY *and* JANICE *leave his car and they both enter the building. The night passes and dawn arrives.*

INT. PAULIE'S HOUSE. DAY

Relatives and friends are paying a Sunday visit. HENRY *and* KAREN *arrive with their two-year-old daughter and new baby. The women make a great fuss over the baby.*

PAULIE'S WIFE: Ohh. Darling!

KAREN: Hi, Phyllis. How are you? How are you?

PAULIE'S WIFE: Come on in.

KAREN: Hi, Paulie.

(*They kiss.*)

PAULIE: Hi. How are you?

KAREN: How are you?

PAULIE: (*To Karen's shy daughter*) No? Not even for Uncle Paulie? (*He laughs.*)

KAREN: A little kiss?

PAULIE: Hi. How you doing?

HENRY: Hi. Hi, ya. Hey.

TUDDY: Hi, yeah, boy. What's happening, Henry? Paulie, let's eat.

PAULIE: We ate yesterday.

TUDDY: Okay.

(PAULIE *laughs.*)

PETE THE KILLER: How are you?

HENRY: Hi, Pete. How you doing?

PETE: How you been?

(PAULIE *talks to* HENRY *aside.*)

PAULIE: What did you hear about that thing?

HENRY: What thing? The Brooklyn thing?

PAULIE: No, no. The guy from downtown.

HENRY: The guy from near where Christie used to live? There?

PAULIE: No. The guy who disappeared up the block from Christie. The one they made the beef on.

HENRY: Oh, yeah, yeah, yeah.

PAULIE: You know the guy I mean?

HENRY: Yeah, yeah, I know, yeah, yeah.

PAULIE: Well, that's, his name was Batts and his people are driving everybody crazy looking for him. They should leave him wherever the fuck he is.

HENRY: N-Nobody knows what happened to him. Uh, uh, he came into the joint that one night and then he just disappeared. That was it.

PAULIE: All right, keep your eyes open, 'cause they're busting my balls about this bastard, all right?

HENRY: Okay.

PAULIE: All right?

HENRY: Yeah.

PAULIE: Yeah.

(*They return to the party.*)

Okay, everybody. Let's eat.

62

INT. THE SUITE. NIGHT

HENRY *and* JANICE *are drinking with friends.* MORRIE *is sorting out a debt.*

CARBONE: *Mara biu.*[1]

CARBONE'S FRIEND: *Te giuro me ne futto.*[2]

MORRIE: Frank, the minga, the binga and you swear, and everything else like this, I want my money.

CARBONE'S FRIEND: *Te giuro me ne futto.*

MORRIE: *Una minuta.* I want my money, he owes it. Otherwise, pitch baseball cards, kids. Frankie, he owes me two hundred bucks.

CARBONE: Ohh. Don't worry about it, all right? You're making a big deal out of nothing.

JIMMY: Henry. Henry. Henry! Henry!
(JIMMY *takes* HENRY *aside.*)

JIMMY: We got a real problem. You know that thing we took care of upstate?

HENRY: Paulie was just talking about that.

JIMMY: We gotta get it out of there.

HENRY: What?

JIMMY: Yeah, we got to get it out of there. They just sold the property and they want to make it into condominiums.

HENRY: Jimmy, it's been six months.

JIMMY: I don't care how long it's been. We got to get it out of there right away.

EXT. THE CONNECTICUT WOODLANDS. NIGHT

HENRY, JIMMY *and* TOMMY *are digging with shovels to find* BATT's *corpse.* HENRY *is sickened by the stench, but the others don't appear to be bothered.*

TOMMY: Hey, Hendry, Hendry, hurry up, will you? My mother's gonna make some fried peppers and sausage for us. Oh, hey, Henry, Henry. Here's an arm.

HENRY: Very funny, guys.

1 Sicilian for 'I'll get angry.'
2 Sicilian for 'I swear, I don't care.'

TOMMY: Hey, here's a leg. Here's a wing. (*He laughs.*) Hey, what do you like, the leg or the wing, Henry? Or do you still go for the old hearts and lungs?
    (HENRY *vomits.*)
HENRY: Oh, that's so bad.
    (TOMMY *and* JIMMY *laugh at* HENRY.)

EXT. HENRY AND KAREN'S HOUSE. DAY

HENRY *is busy hosing out the trunk of his car.* KAREN *passes by with their daughters, and notices the stench.*
KAREN: Come on, girls. Come on.
JUDY: What happened there?
KAREN: Henry, what happened to the car?
HENRY: Ahh. Go, both of you. I hit a skunk, Karen, all right?
KAREN: Come on. Come on. Come on.
HENRY: Go with your mother.
KAREN: Ooh, it's disgusting, Henry!

INT. JANICE'S APARTMENT. NIGHT

JANICE *is showing off her new apartment to her girlfriends, including* SANDY *and* LINDA. HENRY, TOMMY *and other wiseguys are present.*
HENRY: (*Voice-over*) I set up Janice in an apartment around the corner from The Suite. That way I was able to stay over a couple of nights a week.
JANICE: Look at my new antique lamp.
HENRY: (*Voice-over*) Karen was home with the kids and she never asked any questions, anyway.
JANICE: It's all Maurice Valencia.
SANDY: Looks like Roma.
JANICE: This is all silk. This is from Siam. Come on. Come see my bedroom. Tommy, can you please? (*She hands* TOMMY *her dog.*)
TOMMY: Of course. Yeah, I'm gonna eat this dog tonight.
JANICE: Love that crystal ball, or what?
LINDA: It's great.
    (*They enter the bedroom.*)
JANICE: (*Indicating the king-size bed*) Now, this is where we spend most of our time.

LINDA: (*Chuckles*) Nice.

SANDY: I love that floral arrangement.

LINDA: Yeah, great.

JANICE: I got it all at Bonwit Teller.

SANDY: (*Testing a perfume bottle*) French.

HENRY: (*Voice-over*) Janice and I were having so much fun, she started screwing up at work and I had to straighten out her boss a little bit.

INT. THE BACKROOM OF A BRIDAL SHOP. DAY

HENRY *is strangling the* BRIDAL SHOP OWNER *while* TOMMY *and* JIMMY *are beating someone up.*

HENRY: Fucking Janice can do whatever she wants to do! You got it?

BRIDAL SHOP OWNER: (*Gasping*) I got it.

HENRY: Got it?

BRIDAL SHOP OWNER: I got it!

JIMMY: You understand? You hang up once more and you're gonna deal with me, huh!

INT. JANICE'S APARTMENT

HENRY *lifts* JANICE *off her feet and dives with her on to the bed. Her girlfriends scream and laugh.*

JANICE: You're an animal.

    (*One by one they leave the room. As* SANDY *leaves, she and* HENRY *exchange charged looks.*)

INT. THE BASEMENT OF THE SUITE. NIGHT

HENRY, JIMMY, TOMMY *and others are playing cards.* TOMMY *is a little drunk.* SPIDER, *a twenty-two-year-old apprentice hood, is serving them with drinks.*

TOMMY: Hey, Spider! On your way over here, bring me a Cutty and water, huh?

JIMMY: What do you want?

STABILE: I'm good, Tom.

JIMMY: Okay.

HENRY: Two.

JIMMY: What do you want?

TOMMY: I'll play these.

STABILE: What?

CARBONE: You're gonna play those?

TOMMY: What, do I fucking stutter? I'll play those, yeah. (*To* SPIDER.) What am I, a mirage?

SPIDER: What?

TOMMY: What? Where's my fucking drink? I asked you for a drink!

SPIDER: You wanted a drink?

TOMMY: I just asked you for a fucking drink.

SPIDER: No, I thought, I thought you said that you were, 'All right, Spider.'

TOMMY: No, no, no, no. No, no, no, no, no. Where do you got me? On a fucking pay no mind list, kid?

SPIDER: No. 'Cause that – No, I heard, I thought I heard someone say something, 'Spider, Spider'. I thought it was Henry, you know . . .

TOMMY: Spider, Spider. You know, you're a fucking mumbling stuttering little fuck, you know that?

SPIDER: I thought you said it was, 'I was all right, Spider'. So you –

TOMMY: (*Interrupting*) Well, you ain't all right, Spider. You got a lot of fucking problems.

SPIDER: No, I thought you said you were, 'All right, Spider'.

TOMMY: I am all right! You ain't all right, you little fucking prick.

SPIDER: That's what – I thought, I thought I am, that you said –

TOMMY: 'I thought, I thought.' You've been doing this all night to me, you motherfucker!

SPIDER: You wants a drink now? I'll get – I'll bring it for you.

TOMMY: Yeah! Go get me a fucking drink! Move it, you little prick! You walk like fucking Step-and Fetchit! Everybody else you'll fucking run! Run for me, you prick! Dance! Dance the fucking drink back here! The little prick! Hey, what's that movie that Bogart made?

JIMMY: Come on, play.

STABILE: Which one?

TOMMY: The one in which he played a cowboy. The only good one.

STABILE: Oh, the, 'The Oklahoma Kid'.

JIMMY: 'Shane'?

TOMMY: 'The Oklahoma Kid'! 'Shane?' (*Everyone laughs.*) Oklahoma Kid, that's me! I'm the Oklahoma Kid! (*He takes out his gun and waves it in the air.*) You fucking varmint. (*To* SPIDER.) Dance!

JIMMY: What the fuck's the matter with you?

TOMMY: Dance! Yahoo, you motherfucker!

HENRY: Come on.

TOMMY: Round up those fucking wagons! Come on, you motherfucker!

STABILE AND CARBONE: Whoa!

TOMMY: Dance! Dance, you fuck, ya! Dance, you little prick. (TOMMY *shoots at the floor and hits* SPIDER *in the foot.*)

HENRY: Shit! Tommy!

STABILE: Henry, what happened?

HENRY: (*Goes to help* SPIDER) You got him in the foot, Tommy!

SPIDER: Ahh, my foot.

TOMMY: He's fucking fine. All right, so he got shot in the foot! What is it, a big fucking deal?

HENRY: He needs a fucking doctor.

JIMMY: Oh for cry – Come on. Come on.

HENRY: What? Vito. Vito, get a towel.

CARBONE: Nice fucking game.

STABILE: Nice.

CARBONE: Nice fucking game.

HENRY: Do you think he can –

TOMMY: Hey, take him to Ben Casey, the little prick!

JIMMY: Come on.

TOMMY: Walk! Let him crawl there like he crawls for the fucking drinks.

JIMMY: Take him down to Doc. Take him to the doctor down the street.

TOMMY: Fuck him.

SPIDER: Bones are all shattered.

JIMMY: Come on.

TOMMY: Don't get me upset now!

67

JIMMY: Come on, let's go. Play, let's go.

CARBONE: What the fuck. Come on, man.

TOMMY: Don't make a big thing out of it, Spider! You little prick!

JIMMY: Spider.

VITO: Come on.

TOMMY: You're trying to make me think what the fuck I did here! It's an accident. Fuck him. Little fucking actor.

SPIDER: Shit!

TOMMY: He's a little prick.

JIMMY: You in or not?

TOMMY: Yeah, I'm in.

JIMMY: Eight hundred.

TOMMY: Eight hundred!

STABILE: Eight hundred it'll cost you.

JIMMY: Eight hundred.

CARBONE: Eight hundred.

INT. HENRY AND KAREN'S HOUSE. EVENING

HENRY *and* KAREN *are having a row.*

KAREN: You haven't been home in two weeks, Henry. You're not going out tonight! (*She throws his car keys out of the window.*)

HENRY: Hey! Say, hey. Karen, will you grow up? I'm still gonna go out!

KAREN: Not without your car keys, you're not!

HENRY: Are you nuts? Is that it? Are you fucking nuts? What's your problem?

KAREN: Yes, I'm nuts! Something's going on!

HENRY: Stop with that, already.

KAREN: No.

HENRY: Enough! Stop with that!

KAREN: No! I'm telling you, I look in your face and I know that you're lying! (HENRY *throws a lamp at* KAREN. *She screams.*) Get out!

HENRY: Shut up.

KAREN: Get out! Get out of my life!

HENRY: You're fucked up in the head, Karen. This is all in your mind.

KAREN: You're a lousy bastard!

HENRY: You got a problem.

KAREN: Go ahead. Go to your ready-made whores! That's all you're good for! Get out of my life! I can't stand you! (HENRY *storms out.*)

INT. THE BASEMENT OF THE SUITE. NIGHT

Another card game is in progress. SPIDER *is serving drinks, limping with a bandaged foot.*

HENRY: What do you got there? Go, Jim. Good-bye, Jimmy. (*He laughs.*) Spider, what's your rush?

STABILE: Spider, I need some ice.

TOMMY: Fuckin' Drop-along Cassidy.

SPIDER: There you go.

HENRY: Thank you, Spider.

TOMMY: Hey, Spider, that fuckin' bandage on your foot is bigger than you fucking head, you know that?

JIMMY: All right, Spider.

SPIDER: Thank you, sir.

TOMMY: The next thing you know, he's gonna be coming in with one of those fuckin' walkers. Even though you got that, you could dance, huh? Give us a little, give us a-a couple of fucking steps here, Spider. You fucking bullshitter, you. Tell the truth. You're looking for sympathy, is that it, sweetie?

SPIDER: Why don't you go fuck yourself, Tommy?

(*This retort provokes surprise and laughter at the table.*)

JIMMY: I didn't fuckin' hear right. (*Laughing.*) I can't believe what I just heard. Hey, Spider, here. Here, this is for you. Atta boy. I got a respect for this kid. He's got a lot of fuckin' balls, this kid. Good for you. Don't take no shit off nobody. Do you believe this? He shoots him in the foot, he tells him to go fuck himself. Tommy, you gonna let him get away with that? Are you gonna let this fuckin' punk get away with that? What's the matter with you? What's the world comin' to?

(*The players are all laughing loudly.* SPIDER *proudly stands by the bar. Without warning, a furious* TOMMY *pulls out his gun and puts six deafening shots into Spider's chest.*)

TOMMY: That's what the fuckin' world is coming to. How do you like that? How's that? All right?

JIMMY: What's the fuckin' matter with you? What the, what is the fuckin' matter with you? What, are you stupid or what? Tommy. Tommy. I'm kidding with you. What the fuck are you doing? Are you a fucking sick maniac?

TOMMY: Well, who the fuck – How do I know if you're kidding? What do you mean, you're kidding? You're breaking my fucking balls!

JIMMY: I'm, I'm, I'm fucking kidding with you! You fucking shoot the guy?

HENRY: (*Beside* SPIDER's *body*) He's dead.

TOMMY: Good shot. What do you want from me? A good shot.

STABILE: Well, how could you miss at this distance?

TOMMY: What, you got a problem with what I did, Anthony?

70

STABILE: Oh, no. No.

JIMMY: Hey.

TOMMY: Fuckin' rat, anyway. His whole family's all rats. He
would'a grown up to be a rat.

JIMMY: This is stupid. Stupid bastard! I can't fuckin' believe
you. Now you're gonna dig the fuckin' thing up. You're
gonna dig the hole. You're gonna do it. I got no fucking
lime. You're gonna do it.

TOMMY: Who the fuck cares? I'll dig the fuckin' hole. Uh, where
are the shovels?

INT. LOBBY. JANICE'S APARTMENT BUILDING. DAY

KAREN *is pressing* JANICE's *intercom buzzer while her two children* *watch. In her apartment,* JANICE *cowers in fear.*

JANICE: Hello?

KAREN: Hello?

JANICE: Hello?

KAREN: This is Karen Hill. I want to talk to you. Hello? Hello? Don't hang up on me! I want to talk to you. You keep away from my husband, you hear me? Hello? Open the door! Answer me! (*She presses all the buzzers.*) I'm gonna tell everyone who walks in this building that in 2-R, Rossi, you are nothing but a whore! (*She picks up the house phone.*) Is this the superintendent? Yes, I want you to know, sir, that you have a whore living in 2-R, Rossi, Janice Rossi, do you hear me? (KAREN *is now at screaming pitch.*) He's my husband! Get your own goddamn man!

INT. THE BEDROOM IN HENRY AND KAREN'S HOUSE. NIGHT

HENRY *wakes up. Pointed directly at his face is a gun held by a* *hysterical* KAREN, *sitting astride him on the bed.*

KAREN: Wake up, Henry.

HENRY: Karen. What are you doing? Karen, what, are you crazy?

KAREN: I am crazy. And I'm crazy enough to kill the both of you.

HENRY: Karen, take it easy. Okay?

KAREN: Do you love her? Do you? (*Sobbing.*) Do you?

HENRY: Karen, Karen. I love you. You know I love you.

KAREN: No, you don't.

HENRY: Shh. Shh. Shh. Shh. Shh. Shh. Karen, please.

KAREN: No, you don't.

HENRY: (*Whispering*) Just – Just take it easy. Easy.

KAREN: (*Voice-over*) But still I couldn't hurt him. How could I hurt him? I couldn't even bring myself to leave him. The truth was that no matter how bad I felt I was still very attracted to him. Why should I give him to someone else? Why should she win?

HENRY: Karen. Just put it down. You know I love you, don't you. You're all I want, Karen. Please, put the gun down, Karen. Baby, come on. Shh. Shh.

(HENRY *quickly moves his head away, grabs the gun from*
KAREN *and slaps her across the face, knocking her off the bed.*)

HENRY: What, are you fucking crazy, Karen? (*He holds the gun at
her face.*)

KAREN: No. Stop it!

HENRY: Are you crazy? Huh? I got enough to worry about getting
fucking whacked on the street. I gotta fuckin' – Huh?

KAREN: (*Yelling*) I'm sorry.

HENRY: I gotta fuckin' come home? For this? I should fuckin' kill
you! How does it feel?

KAREN: I'm sorry. (*Sobbing*.) I'm sorry.

HENRY: Huh? Huh? How does it feel, Karen? Who the fuck am I
kidding?
(HENRY *leaves the apartment.*)

KAREN: I'm sorry!

INT. JANICE'S APARTMENT. DAY

HENRY *opens the door and* PAULIE *and* JIMMY *enter.*

HENRY: Hey.

JIMMY: Hey.

HENRY: How are you doing?

JANICE: Hi, Jimmy! How are you?

JIMMY: Hi, how are you doing?
(*They kiss.*)
Lookin' good.

JANICE: Thank you. Good to see you.

JIMMY: Good to see you.

JANICE: Hi, Paulie.

PAULIE: Hi, honey.
(*They kiss.*)
How are ya?

JANICE: Good.

HENRY: Um, why don't you go get me some cigarettes, okay?

JANICE: Sure. Does anyone need anything?

HENRY: No, we're all right. (*To* PAULIE.) Do you want anything
to drink? Beer or – ?

PAULIE: No, no. No, this . . .

JIMMY: No, I'm all right.

HENRY: Chinese food?

JIMMY: No.

(JANICE *leaves them*.)

PAULIE: No. Come on, sit down.

JIMMY: Sit down.

PAULIE: Karen came to the house. She's very upset. This is no good. You got to straighten this thing out.

JIMMY: We got to have calm now. You understand? With her we don't know what the hell she's gonna do. She's getting all hysterical. She gets very excited.

PAULIE: She's wild. And you, you gotta take it easy. You got children. I'm not saying you got to go back to her this minute, but you gotta go back. I mean, it's the only way. You got to keep up appearances.

JIMMY: Yeah, I mean, I got the two of them coming over to the house every day, commiserating. The two of them. I can't have it. I can't have it. You know, I just, I can't do it, Henry. You know, it's – it's a – I can't do it.

PAULIE: Nobody says that you can't do what you want to do.

JIMMY: No, do what you want to do. We all know that, I mean . . . This is what it is, okay? We know what it is.

PAULIE: But you have to do what's right.

JIMMY: You have to go home to the family, you understand? You gotta go home. Okay? Look at me. You gotta go home. Smarten up. All right?

HENRY: Yeah.

PAULIE: All right. I'm gonna talk to Karen. I'll straighten this thing out. I know just what to say to her. Okay? I'm gonna tell her you're gonna go back to her and everything's gonna be just the way it was when you were first married. You're gonna romance her. It's gonna be beautiful. I know how to talk to her, especially to her. In the meantime Jimmy and Tommy are going down to Tampa this weekend to pick something up for me. Instead, you go with Jimmy.

JIMMY: Yeah, you come with me and we'll go down there, okay?

PAULIE: Have a good time. Take some time for yourself. Relax. Sit in the sun. Take a couple of days off.

HENRY: All right.

JIMMY: We'll have a good time.

74

PAULIE: Enjoy yourselves. And when you come back, you'll go back to Karen. Huh?

HENRY: Okay.

PAULIE: Please, there's no other way. You're not gonna get a divorce. We're not *animali*.

JIMMY: They're not gonna get a divorce. She'll never divorce him. She'll kill him, but she won't divorce him.

PAULIE: (*Chuckles*) Yeah. Yeah. (HENRY *laughs too*.) There.

INT. REAR SEAT OF CAR. NIGHT

Tampa, Florida, two days later

JIMMY *and* HENRY *are beating up a* BOOKIE.

JIMMY: All right, you gonna pay it?

BOOKIE: I ain't got it, I swear.

JIMMY: What?

　　(*The* BOOKIE *grunts*.)

　　Huh? You gonna pay?

HENRY: Just give us the fucking money!

JIMMY: Huh?

BOOKIE: I can't. I – I can't, I swear.

JIMMY: Let's go. Let's go!

EXT. TAMPA CITY ZOO. NIGHT

HENRY *and* JIMMY *threaten to throw the* BOOKIE *into the lions' den*.

JIMMY: Come on. We'll throw the bastard to the lions.

BOOKIE: No! No!

HENRY: What fucking lions? I ain't going near any lions, Jimmy!

JIMMY: We'll throw him over the moat.

BOOKIE: No! No!

　　(*They hold the* BOOKIE *by his legs over the fence*.)

HENRY: (*Voice-over*) They must really feed each other to the lions down there, because the guy gave the money right up.

BOOKIE: I swear to Christ I'll get the money.

HENRY: (*Voice-over*) And we got to spend the rest of the weekend at the track.

EXT. A ROADSIDE PHONE BOOTH. NIGHT

The BOOKIE *is on the phone while* HENRY *and* JIMMY *wait outside.*

BOOKIE: Yeah. They mean business. Don't tell me about that, they almost threw me to the goddamn lions! Yeah!

HENRY: (*Voice-over*) Then, I couldn' believe what happened. When we got home we were all over the newspaper.

INT. GOVERNMENT OFFICE. DAY

The BOOKIE'S SISTER *is surrounded by FBI men.*

HENRY: (*Voice-over*) At first, I didn't even know why we got picked up. Then I found out that the guy we roughed up turned out to have a sister working as a typist for the FBI. Who could believe it. Of all the fucking people!

BOOKIE'S SISTER: You should have seen his face. It was so badly beaten. I mean, I never saw so much blood in – They wanted him dead. I'm sure of it. I'm scared of them myself. (*Photographs of* HENRY *and* JIMMY *being arrested, as well as the* BOOKIE.)

HENRY: (*Voice-over*) She gave up everybody. Jimmy. Me. Even her brother.

INT. A COURTROOM. DAY

HENRY *and* JIMMY *are standing before a* JUDGE.

HENRY: (*Voice-over*) It took the jury six hours to bring us in guilty. The judge gave Jimmy and me ten years like he was giving away candy.

JUDGE: . . . ten years in a federal penitentiary. You will now be turned over to the United States Attorney General's Office.

INT. MAXWELL'S PLUM BAR. LATE AFTERNOON

HENRY *is being treated to a farewell drink.* KAREN *stands apart, crying.*

MORRIE: Well, sweet Henry . . . Toast, guys. Good trip, good life, get out soon. Good trip, sweetheart. Tell us if you need us.

STABILE: Call us if you need us.

MORRIE: We'll watch the home front.

CARBONE: *Statti buono*, huh?[1]

TOMMY: Say hello to those blow job hacks, huh? (*Everyone laughs.*) Don't forget, motherfuck them every chance you get, Hendry.

HENRY: I love you. I'll call you, uh, when I get the chance.

(HENRY *walks out of the bar to a limo waiting at the curb, and gets in the rear seat. He downs a palm full of valium.*)

HENRY: Now take me to jail.

INT. A DORMITORY IN LEWISBURG FEDERAL PRISON

PAULIE, VINNIE *and* JOHNNY DIO *are busy preparing food as if they were in their kitchens at home.*

HENRY: (*Voice-over*) In prison, dinner was always a big thing. We had a pasta course and then we had a meat or a fish.

(PAULIE *is slicing garlic very thinly with a razor blade.*)

HENRY: (*Voice-over*) Paulie did the prep work. He was doing a year for contempt, and he had this wonderful system for doing the garlic. He used a razor and he used to slice it so thin that it used to liquify in a pan with just a little oil. It's a very good system. Vinnie was in charge of the tomato sauce.

VINNIE: Get that smell?

JOHNNY DIO: I got that smell.

VINNIE: We got . . . there's three kinds of meat in the meatballs.

JOHNNY DIO: What did you put in it?

VINNIE: We got . . . veal, beef and pork.

JOHNNY DIO: Ah, good. But you got to have the pork.

VINNIE: Oh, that's – that's – that's the flavor.

JOHNNY DIO: Pork is the real flavor. You can have all the . . .

HENRY: (*Voice-over*) I-I felt he used too many onions, but it was still a very good sauce.

PAULIE: Vinnie, don't put too many onions in the sauce.

VINNIE: I didn't put too much onions in, uh, Paul. There are three small onions, that's all I did.

JOHNNY DIO: Three onions? How many cans of tomatoes you put in there?

VINNIE: I put two cans, two big cans.

1 Sicilian for 'Stay well, huh?'

JOHNNY DIO: You don't need three onions.

HENRY: (*Voice-over*) Johnny Dio did the meat. We didn't have a broiler, so Johnny did everything in pans.

JOHNNY DIO: Paulie! How do you want your steak today?

PAULIE: Well done.

HENRY: (*Voice-over*) It used to smell up the joint something awful and the hacks used to die, but he still cooked a great steak.

JOHNNY DIO: Vinnie, how do you like yours?

VINNIE: Rare. Medium rare.

JOHNNY DIO: Medium rare. Hmm, an aristocrat.

HENRY: (*Voice-over*) See, you know when you think of prison, you get pictures in your mind of all those old movies with rows and rows of guys behind bars.

(*A box marked 'Perishable Fresh Seafood – Keep Iced' is brought in.*)

GUARD: Vinnie, here's your lobsters.

VINNIE: Okay, thanks.

HENRY: (*Voice-over*) But it wasn't like that for wiseguys. It really wasn't that bad. Excepting that I missed Jimmy. He was doing his time in Atlanta.

JOHNNY DIO: Vinnie, give me two steaks while you're in there, all right?

VINNIE: Okay, John.

JOHNNY DIO: Sure enough, she goes in . . .

HENRY: (*Voice-over*) I mean, everybody else in the joint was doing real time, all mixed together, living like pigs. But we lived alone. And we owned the joint.

JOHNNY DIO: . . . baseball-batted them two sons-of-bitches.

VINNIE: Sure.

JOHNNY DIO: You couldn't recognize them.

VINNIE: Good. They deserved it.

HENRY: (*Voice-over*) Even the hacks we couldn't bribe would never rat on the guys that we did.

JOHNNY DIO: But that's the way it should still be. Then the neighbourhood had respect. People loved one another. You left your doors open.

VINNIE: That's right.

(HENRY *comes in carrying a heavy canvas mail sack.*)

HENRY: Sorry it took so long. That skinny guard's getting to be a

78

real pain in the ass.

PAULIE: Yeah, we're gonna have to do something about that bastard.

HENRY: No, I-I took care of him.

PAULIE: All right, what'd you bring?

HENRY: (*Emptying the sack of booze and food*) All right, uh, some bread.

PAULIE: Good. Fresh.

HENRY: Vinnie, I got your peppers and onions, salami, prosciutto, a lot'a cheese.

PAULIE: Come on. Come on. What else.

HENRY: Scotch.

PAULIE: Nice.

HENRY: Uh, here's some red wine.

PAULIE: Okay. Now we could eat.

HENRY: Red. I got some white too.

PAULIE: Give me the white too. Beautiful.

HENRY: All right.

PAULIE: Okay, boys, let's eat. Come on. It's ready, Vinnie.

VINNIE: Coming up.

HENRY: Here's some more bread.
   (*They all sit down to eat.*)

PAULIE: Tomorrow we eat sangdwiches. You got to go on a diet, Vinnie. Believe me. (*Chuckles.*) Johnny?

VINNIE: There ya go.

PAULIE: *Nu poco 'e vino.*[1]

HENRY: *Salut'.*
   (*After the meal, they sit round and play cards.* HENRY, *unseen by the others, fills his pockets with drugs from the sack.*)

PAULIE: Read 'em and weep. What are ya doin'?

JOHNNY: Vinnie, you took my card.

VINNIE: It's a diamond.

JOHNNY: Take that.

PAULIE: Yeah, I'll take that. Hey. Get rid of 'em. I'm tired of losin' here.

HENRY: All right, I'll catch you guys later.

PAULIE: Yeah. What, are you going for a walk in the park?

1 Sicilian for 'Have a little wine.'

INT. PRISON GUARDS' BOOTH, VISITING ROOM. DAY

In a Prison Guard's booth, while his back is deliberately turned,
HENRY *is dealing out drugs.*

HENRY: Okay, here you go.

DRUG BUYER: 'Kay. I'll catch you next week.

HENRY: Good.

DRUG BUYER: All right.

HENRY: Thanks, Tony.

DRUG BUYER: All right.

PRISON GUARD: Are there any more?

HENRY: No, that's it. Have a good weekend. Thanks.

PRISON GUARD: (*Accepting money from* HENRY) Thank you,
    Henry.

INT. PRISON VISITOR'S GATE. DAY

Visiting time. The camera tracks by wives and girlfriends talking to
PRISONERS. LAWYERS *are also present.*

FIRST PRISONER: (*Being given oral sex*) Uhh.

SECOND PRISONER: I know. We gotta be patient.

THIRD PRISONER: Are you my lawyer or not?

LAWYER: I'm your lawyer.

THIRD PRISONER: Well, then work for me! Why should they be
    on the street, free?
    (*Wearing an over-sized coat for smuggling booze, food and drugs,*
    KAREN *arrives with her two daughters. The* GUARDS *let her*
    by-pass the usual security checks.)

FIRST GUARD: Miss Hill, come here.

KAREN: Come on. You girls stay right here. I want you to hold
    hands.

FIRST GUARD: Okay, go right up to the front there.

KAREN: Together. Let's go.

SECOND GUARD: Come on, sweetheart. We'll get 'em for you.
    Come on. How you doin', Miz Hill?

KAREN: Good. How are you?

SECOND GUARD: Very well, thank you.
    (*In the visitor's book,* KAREN *sees the name 'Janice Rossi'*
    written next to 'Hill, Henry'. Seated in the large gymnasium

where PRISONERS *meet their wives and children,* KAREN
becomes angry with HENRY.)

HENRY: What are you talking about?

KAREN: I saw her name in the register.

HENRY: Jesus Christ, Karen.

KAREN: You want her to visit you? Let her stay up all night
crying and writing letters to the parole board.

HENRY: What am I doing here? Where am I? I'm in jail! I can't
stop people from coming to see me!

KAREN: Good. Let her sneak this stuff in for you every week.
(*She starts unloading the food, booze and drugs hidden in her
coat. Although she is making a lot of noise and becoming very
visible, the* GUARD *tries not to notice.*)

HENRY: Come on.

KAREN: Let her fight with those creep bastards every week!

HENRY: Look – Look what you're doing! Look what you're
doing! Stop it! Shh.

KAREN: I'm sorry. Let her sneak this shit in for you, Henry.

HENRY: Stop it. Will you stop it, Karen? Will you stop it?

KAREN: Let her do it! Let her do it!
(RUTH *begins to cry.*)

HENRY: Shh. Shh. Shh. Shh. Ruth, Ruth, Ruth, come here.
Come on, baby. Shh.

KAREN: Nobody's helping me. I am all alone. Belle and Morrie
are broke.

HENRY: It's okay.

KAREN: I asked your friend Remo for the money that he owes
you. You know what he told me? He told me to take my kids
to the police station and get on welfare.

HENRY: Karen, it is gonna be okay.

KAREN: Even Paulie, since he got out, I never see him. I never see
anybody anymore.

HENRY: It's only you and me. That's what happens when you go
away. I've told you that. We're on our own. Forget
everybody else. Forget Paulie. You know, as long as he's on
parole he doesn't want anybody doing anything.
(RUTH *continues to cry.*)
Shh. Shh. Shh. Shh. Shh. Shh. Shh.

KAREN: I can't do it.

HENRY: Shh. yes, you can, Karen. Listen to me. All I need from
 you is to keep bringing me this stuff. I got a guy in here from
 Pittsburgh who's gonna help me move it. Believe me, in a
 month we're gonna be fine. We won't need anybody.

KAREN: I'm afraid. I'm afraid if Paulie finds out.

HENRY: What'd I just say? Don't worry about him. He is not
 helping us out. Is he putting any food on the table? We've
 got to help each other. We've just gotta – Listen, we gotta be
 really, really careful while we do it.

KAREN: I don't want to hear a word about her anymore, Henry –

HENRY: Never.

EXT. PRISON GATE. DAY

Four years later

HENRY *leaves the prison gate in civilian clothes. Waiting for him by their car is* KAREN. HENRY *and* KAREN *embrace.*

INT. KAREN'S SMALL APARTMENT

They enter Karen's cramped, sparse apartment.

JUDY: Oh, we missed you.

RUTH: Are you here to stay?

JUDY: Did you see our pictures? I did the one with the house and rainbow.

RUTH: I did the sun.

JUDY: My chorus concert is in two weeks. Are you coming? Do you like the house?

HENRY: (*Shocked by the loss in personal comforts*) Karen, get packed. We're moving out of here.

JUDY: Why?

KAREN: With what?

HENRY: Don't worry with that. You just start looking for a new house, okay? I gotta go to Pittsburgh in the morning. Those guys out there, they owe me fifteen grand. We'll be all right. I got things lined up.

KAREN: Pittsburgh? You have to go see your parole officer tomorrow.

HENRY: Karen, don't worry about it. Everything's gonna be fine. Who wants to go to Uncle Paulie's?

RUTH *and* JUDY: Me!

HENRY: Huh?

INT. PAULIE'S HOUSE. DAY

Platters of food are brought out of the kitchen and placed on the table.
HENRY, KAREN *and their daughters are welcomed back amongst their old friends. There's a lot of chatter and activity.*

HENRY: You hungry?

PAULIE: No, he's an arrogant guy. He didn't do the right thing.

KAREN: (*To* JUDY) What? What do you want?

PHYLLIS: Sweetheart, let Mommy eat, huh?

PAULIE: Here. You look good. You ate good. Did we eat this good in the joint?

(PAULIE *takes* HENRY *outside.*)

I don't want any more of that shit.

HENRY: What shit? What are you talking about?

PAULIE: Just stay away from the garbage, you know what I mean.

HENRY: What? Paulie, what are you –

PAULIE: (*Interrupting*) I'm not talking about what you did inside. You did what you had to do. I'm talking about now. From now, here and now.

HENRY: Paulie, why would I want to get into that?

PAULIE: Don't make a jerk out'a me. Just don't do it. Just don't do it. Now I want to talk to you about Jimmy. You gotta

84

watch out for him. He's a good earner, but he's wild. Takes too many chances.

HENRY: Yeah, I know that, I know Jimmy. Do you think I would take chances like Jimmy?

PAULIE: And Tommy. He's a good kid too, but he's crazy. He's a cowboy. He's got too much to prove.

HENRY: No, I know –

PAULIE: (*Interrupting*) You've got to watch out for kids like this.

HENRY: Yeah, I know what they are. I-I only use them for certain things. So listen, you don't have to worry –

PAULIE: (*Interrupting*) Listen, I ain't gonna get fucked like Gribbs, you understand? Gribbs is seventy years old and the fucking guy's gonna die in prison. I don't need that. So I'm warning everybody. Everybody. Could be my son, could be anybody. Gribbs got twenty years just for saying hello to some fuck who was sneakin' behind his back selling junk. I don't need that. Ain't gonna happen to me, you understand?

HENRY: Uh-huh.

PAULIE: You know that you're only out early 'cause I got you a job.

HENRY: Yeah.

PAULIE: And I don't need this heat, understand that?

HENRY: Uh-huh.

PAULIE: And you see anybody fucking around with this shit you're gonna tell me, right?

HENRY: Yeah.

PAULIE: (*He slaps* HENRY) That means anybody.

HENRY: All right.

PAULIE: Yeah?

HENRY: Yeah. Yeah, of course.

HENRY: (*Voice-over*) It took me about a week of sneaking around before I could unload the Pittsburgh stuff, but when I did it was a real score.

INT. SANDY'S APARTMENT. DAY

SANDY, *a friend of* JANICE, *who has begun an affair with* HENRY, *is busy cutting cocaine on a table where drugs are jumbled up with old coffee cups, dirty dishes and newspapers.*

85

HENRY: (*Voice-over*) I-I started using Sandy's place to mix the stuff and even with Sandy snorting more than she mixed, I could see that this was a really good business. I-I made twelve thousand dollars in my second week. I had a down payment on my house and things were really rolling. All I had to do was every once in a while tell Sandy that I loved her.

(HENRY *and* SANDY *smoke a cigarette together.*)

HENRY: That's it. That's it. Great.

SANDY: These rocks are so big.

HENRY: Huh. They're nice. Here, you want a puff.

SANDY: Mmm. Sure.

HENRY: You do this really really good. You do, you do, you do.

HENRY: (*Voice-over*) But it was perfect I'm telling you. As long as I kept getting the stuff from Pittsburgh, I knew Paulie would never find out.

INT. A PAROLE OFFICE. DAY

Waiting to see his PAROLE OFFICER, JIMMY *is joined by* TOMMY *and* HENRY, *who shows them a shoe box full of cash from his drug deals.*

HENRY: Here. See? What'd I tell you?

JIMMY: Great.

TOMMY: That's it.

HENRY: (*Voice-over*) Within a couple of weeks it got to be so big I needed some help. So I got Jimmy and Tommy to come in with me.

HENRY: What'd I tell you?

JIMMY: Nice.

TOMMY: It's fuckin' great. What nice?

PAROLE OFFICER: Mister Conway. Good morning.

JIMMY: How you doing?

PAROLE OFFICER: You bring your pay slips?

JIMMY: Yeah.

INT. HENRY AND KAREN'S NEW HOUSE. DAY

KAREN *takes* MORRIE *and his wife* BELLE *on a tour of a wildly over-decorated living room.*

KAREN: Four and a half months of dirt.

BELLE: It's so good.

KAREN: I did it. (*Chuckles.*) Do you love it?

BELLE: It's wonderful.

KAREN: (*Indicating a large leather sofa*) And this we just had to
have made special. Go ahead sit in it, Belle. The others you
couldn't even sit in them.

BELLE: Oh!

KAREN: Okay, you ready? Watch the wall with the rock.
(*At the flick of a switch, a fake rock wall parts in the middle to
reveal a television and hi-fi unit.*)

BELLE: Oh. (*Laughs.*) Karen, that is so . . .

KAREN: The electricians did it special. (*She takes* BELLE *into the
next room.*) Come on. Come on. (*Indicating a large inlaid
table.*) All right, this was imported. It came in two pieces.
Can you believe what they can do? It's unbelievable.

HENRY: See, it's nice, huh?

MORRIE: Henry, Henry, come over here.

HENRY: What?

MORRIE: Did you and Jimmy talk?

HENRY: Yeah. I talked to him and he's looking into everything.

MORRIE: Oh, uh, fucking good. This will make the Air France
haul look like goddamn peanuts, man.

HENRY: Shh! Morrie, come on.

MORRIE: But it's okay, he's gonna do it, right?

HENRY: I just told you. He's gonna check everything out. He's
lookin' into it and we'll see what happens.

MORRIE: Yeah, okay. As long as he's looking into it.

HENRY: No promises.

MORRIE: Yeah, I know, I know, I know. But do you understand?
There's millions in there. And I've been bleeding for this
caper. I've been cultivating this son-of-a-bitch for two years.
He owes me twenty grand. Once in a lifetime. I could retire.
No more nut every week. No more bullshit. Ah, my dream
comes true.

HENRY: Morrie.

MORRIE: Yeah?

HENRY: Let's get a drink.

MORRIE: Okay, babe.

HENRY: Come on.

A seedy bar full of wiseguys. HENRY, TOMMY, JIMMY *and* MORRIE *are watching a baseball game.*

MORRIE: One more shot. Beautiful. That's two on the spread. Never sweat a fix.

JIMMY: Come on, come on, come on, come on. Let's go. Let's go.

HENRY: (*Voice-over*) And these were the guys that Jimmy put together for what turned out to be the biggest heist in American history, the Lufthansa heist.

TOMMY: If they fuck this up I'm gonna blow up Boston. If they lose it now . . . How the fuck can they lose now?

CARBONE: Come on, we're gonna win. Think positive, will you?

HENRY: (*Voice-over*) Tommy and Carbone were gonna grab the outside guard and make him get us in the front door.

FRENCHY: Louisiana Lightning!

JOE: Louisiana *u cazz*![1]

HENRY: (*Voice-over*) Frenchy and Joe Buddha had to round up the workers.

FRENCHY: Come on, Buddha. I'm hot. Come on.

HENRY: (*Voice-over*) Johnny Roastbeef had to keep them all tied up and away from the alarm.

JOHNNY ROASTBEEF: They're making it look good. It's terrific. What a cigar game. This is a lock.

HENRY: (*Voice-over*) Even Stacks Edwards got in on it. He used to hang around the lounge and play guitar. Everybody loved Stacks.

STACKS EDWARDS: (*Wandering into the bar*) Hey, baby. Hey, man, how are you?

HENRY: (*Voice-over*) What he was supposed to do was steal the panel truck and afterwards compact it by a friend of ours out in Jersey.

TOMMY: When are you gonna get that ten thousand from that other joint?

HENRY: (*Voice-over*) Only Morrie was driving us nuts.
     (MORRIE *is pestering* JIMMY *at the bar.*)

MORRIE: Just picture it as like, you know, a little advance.

JIMMY: Come on. Morrie.

[1] Sicilian for 'my ass'.

MORRIE: A little –

JIMMY: (*Interrupting*) Morrie, have a drink and shut up.

MORRIE: A little advance. Come on.

JIMMY: Just shut up, okay.

HENRY: (*Voice-over*) Just because he set this up he felt he could bust Jimmy's balls for an advance on the money we were gonna steal. He didn't mean anything by it, that's just, that's just the way he was.

MORRIE: Just a little advance. You, you give advances on the hijacks, man. Every guy knows that in the street.

HENRY: Morrie, Morrie, let's just watch the game. We're not doing too good with . . .

INT. HENRY AND KAREN'S BEDROOM. DAY

KAREN *and* LOIS, *a friend, are admiring a baby while* HENRY *removes drugs from the baby bag.*

HENRY: (*Voice-over*) I had everybody working for me. Even our old babysitter Lois Byrd.

KAREN: Hello. Hello. Oh, she's so sweet. Hello, little thing.

HENRY: Did you have a good flight?

LOIS: I hate Pittsburgh. Where'd you find such creeps?

HENRY: Oh, come on, they're not that bad.

LOIS: Hi, baby.

HENRY: And it's worth it, isn't it?

KAREN: Is this the same baby you used last week?

LOIS: No, that one was my sister's. This is Deirdra's.

KAREN: Oh.

LOIS: Oh, big yawn.

KARNE: She looks just like you. Lois.

LOIS: Oh, that's what the stewardess said.

KAREN: (*Chuckles*) Yeah.

INT. SANDY'S APARTMENT

The table as before strewn with drugs, scales, mixers, bowls and sieves. HENRY *is busy making 'cokeballs'.* SANDY *offers him a line of cocaine and then takes a snort herself.*

HENRY: Take it easy, Sandy.

SANDY: Come on, Henry. Give me a break. We got enough here to go around.

HENRY: You got all day. Let's make it last, all right? Take it easy.

SANDY: Hey.

HENRY: I gotta go.

SANDY: Where are you goin'? Where are you goin'?

HENRY: Come on. Don't start. You know I gotta go do this thing. Fuck! Where are my keys?

SANDY: They're right there.

HENRY: It's a mess. It's like a pig pen. What do you think I got you a dishwasher for, huh?

SANDY: I hate doing the dishes. It fucks up my nails.

HENRY: I don't care if you hate doing the dishes, you gotta be smart. Look at all this powder around here. There's enough to put us away forever.

SANDY: Henry, Henry, loosen up. (*She begins embracing him.*)

HENRY: Whoa, what are you doing?

SANDY: Come on, come on.

HENRY: I-I-I got to go.

SANDY: No, you don't have to go anywhere. (*She feels him up.*) Make them wait. Make them wait. Come on.
(HENRY *gives in and takes his jacket off.*)

INT. SANDY'S SHOWER

HENRY *is listening to the radio while taking a shower.*

RADIO ANNOUNCER: And nobody knows for sure just how much was taken in the daring pre-dawn raid at the Lufthansa cargo terminal at Kennedy Airport. The FBI says two million dollars, Port Authority police say four million dollars, the city cops say five. Lufthansa has not said anything, but they've promised to break their silence soon with a press conference.

HENRY: (*yelling with joy*) Jim-m-m-my! Those son-of-a-bitches!

RADIO ANNOUNCER: And W.I.N.S. will be there to cover it live from the scene of the heist at J.F.K. It looks like a big one. Maybe the biggest this town has ever seen. Stay tuned.

HENRY: Oh, Jimmy!

INT. ROBERT'S LOUNGE. NIGHT

A private Christmas party is in full swing. In reality it is a Lufthansa victory party. As they arrive, HENRY *and* KAREN *are hugged by* JIMMY.

JIMMY: Hey!

HENRY: Jimmy!

JIMMY: Come here, you!

HENRY: Hey!

JIMMY: Come here! Look at this genius. This genius.

JOHNNY ROASTBEEF: (*Arriving with his* WIFE): Merry Christmas.

HENRY: Tommy.

JOHNNY ROASTBEEF: Merry Christmas, Henry.

HENRY: Hey.

JOHNNY ROASTBEEF: Merry Christmas, Jimmy.

JIMMY: How are you doin', huh?

JOHNNY ROASTBEEF: All right. How are you doing, buddy?

JOHNNY ROASTBEEF'S WIFE: Hi, Merry Christmas.

JIMMY: Hello. Who's this?

JOHNNY ROASTBEEF: Jimmy, this is my wife.

JIMMY: Oh, how you doin', sweetheart?

JOHNNY ROASTBEEF: Jimmy, come here. I want to show you something. Jimmy, come here.

JIMMY: All right, excuse me.

(JOHNNY ROASTBEEF *shows* JIMMY *his new pink Cadillac convertible parked outside the door.*)

JOHNNY ROASTBEEF: Isn't she gorgeous? I bought it for my wife. It's a coupé. I love that car.

JIMMY: Listen to me. What did I tell you before? I talked to you before, didn't I?

JOHNNY ROASTBEEF: Yeah.

JIMMY: Didn't I say what was going on? Didn't I say not to go buy anything for a while?

JOHNNY ROASTBEEF: Yeah, but –

JIMMY: (*Interrupting*) The fucking car. Come on.

JOHNNY ROASTBEEF: It's a wedding gift, Jimmy. It's from my mother. It's under her name. I just got married.

JOHNNY ROASTBEEF'S WIFE: I love that car.

JIMMY: Excuse me, darling, for just a second.

JOHNNY ROASTBEEF: I just got married.

JIMMY: Johnny, are you, are you nuts?

JOHNNY ROASTBEEF: What are you getting excited for, Jimmy?

JIMMY: What's the matter with you? What am I getting excited for? Are you stupid? We got a million fuckin' bulls out there. Everybody's watching us and you get a fuckin' car. And you're telling me I'm excited.

JOHNNY ROASTBEEF: It's under my mother's name. It's a wedding gift.

JIMMY: I don't give a fuck whose name it's under. Are you stupid or what? Didn't you hear what I said? Don't buy anything. Don't get anything. Nothing big. Didn't you hear what I said? What's the matter with you?

JOHNNY ROASTBEEF: I'm sorry, Jimmy. What are you getting excited for, Jimmy?

JIMMY: What am I getting excited about? Because you're going to get us all fuckin' pinched, that's why. What are you, stupid? What's the matter with you?

JOHNNY ROASTBEEF: Excuse me, I apologize.

JIMMY: What's the matter with you?

JOHNNY ROASTBEEF: I'm sorry.

JIMMY: What the fuck is the matter with you?

JOHNNY ROASTBEEF: It's . . . I'm sorry, Jimmy. It's – It's under my mother's name, that's all.

JIMMY: What'd you say?

JOHNNY ROASTBEEF: It's under my mother's name.

JIMMY: (*Very angry now*) Are you being a fucking wiseguy with me?

JOHNNY ROASTBEEF: I'm sorry, Jimmy. I apologize.

JIMMY: What did I tell you? What did I tell you? What did I tell you?

JOHNNY ROASTBEEF: I'm sorry.

JIMMY: You don't buy anything, you hear me? You don't buy anything.

JOHNNY ROASTBEEF: I'm sorry, Jimmy.

JIMMY: The fat fuck. He ought'a wear a sign.

(*Next in walks a smiling* FRANKIE CARBONE, *accompanied by his* WIFE *wearing a very expensive mink coat.*)

CARBONE: Hello, Henry.

JIMMY: What are you, laughing? I can't believe this.

CARBONE: What?

JIMMY: What are you, stupid or what?

(*He starts removing the coat from* CARBONE'S WIFE)

Excuse me, excuse me.

CARBONE: What's the matter?

JIMMY: Take it off. Take it off.

CARBONE: What the fuck's going on here?

CARBONE'S WIFE: Why? What – What's the matter? What's the matter?

JIMMY: Take it off. Take it off.

CARBONE'S WIFE: What's the matter?

JIMMY: Didn't I tell you not to get anything big? Didn't I tell you not to attract attention, huh? In two days one guy gets a fucking Caddy and one gets a twenty-thousand-dollar mink. Bring it back.

CARBONE: All right.

JIMMY: Take your fucking mink.

CARBONE: All right. I'll bring it back.

JIMMY: Bring it back. I don't care what you do with it. Bring it where you got it before. Get it outta here. I don't care. You understand? Get it outta here!

CARBONE: Okay. I heard you. All right. (*To his* WIFE.) Amon nino.[1] *Alesta te.*[2] *Amon nino. Amon nino, Amon nino. Rembre le culunno.*[3] *Alesta te. Amon nino. State stuitu.*[4] Shut the fuck up! Let's go.

(*At the bar,* STACKS EDWARDS *is mixing drinks with his girlfriend.*)

STACKS EDWARDS: This drink here is better than sex, babe.

TOMMY: (*To his current girlfriend,* ROSIE) I'm going to go see Stacks. Don't you fucking look at anybody. Look straight ahead or I'll fucking kill ya.

ILLEANA: He's so jealous. I mean if I even look at anyone else, he'll kill me.

1 Sicilian for 'Let's go.'
2 Sicilian for 'Hurry up.'
3 Sicilian for 'Stop breaking my balls.'
4 Sicilian for 'Shut up.'

MICKEY: That's great.

JIMMY: Do you believe them? I tell them all to relax. Don't attract attention. Act normal. What do they do?

MORRIE: Hey, guys, I've been looking all over for you. Jimmy, Henry, how are you?

HENRY: Hey.

MORRIE: Merry Christmas. Hey, listen, I need the money.

JIMMY: Hey, Morrie, relax. Relax, okay?

MORRIE: Jimmy, I need the money.

JIMMY: It's Christmas, relax. Relax. (*He walks away.*)

MORRIE: I'm relaxing. I need the money. I did what I had to do. I need the money.

HENRY: Not tonight, Morrie.

MORRIE: Hey, listen. I did my caper. He owes me.

HENRY: Come on.

MORRIE: I mean everybody's flashing their stuff here. Evidently they got their money. They're gonna . . . They're wearing it. I'm wearing the same old shit.

HENRY: It's – It's not . . . not tonight.

MORRIE: I got to talk to him. Jimmy. Jimmy. Jimmy.

HENRY: (*Trying to hold him back*) Morrie, Morrie, Morrie, come on.

MORRIE: No, listen, I got five hundred grand coming to me.

HENRY: Morrie, just – Shh. Shh. Shh. Shh.

MORRIE: It's the biggest fucking bundle he ever made in his life.

HENRY: All right. Morrie, I'll go talk to him.

MORRIE: I want my money.

HENRY: I'll go talk to him. Go have a drink, all right?

MORRIE: It's poison to my eyes.

HENRY: I'll talk to him.

MORRIE: Poison to my eyes.

BELLE: Morris, baby, are you all right?

MORRIE: No, I'm not.

BELLE: Come on, sit down.

(*In a backroom,* HENRY *speaks to* JIMMY.)

HENRY: Jimmy. Ah.

JIMMY: (*Giving* HENRY *a stack of bills*) Christmas. Your share. Just a little taste.

HENRY: (*Chuckles*) Jimmy.

JIMMY: We did it. We did it. We did it. We did it. We did it.
HENRY: Yeah.

> (*There is a knock on the door.*)

PETE: (*From outside*) Hey, Jimmy?
JIMMY: Yeah?
PETE: Jimmy?
JIMMY: Yeah, yeah, who is it?
PETE: It's me.
JIMMY: Pete?
PETE: Yeah.
JIMMY: All right, one second. (*To* HENRY.) Don't do what
Frankie and Johnny did. Don't be a moron with your
money. Do what's right. You understand?
HENRY: Yeah, of course.

INT. HENRY AND KAREN'S HOUSE. NIGHT

HENRY *comes in carrying a huge artificial Christmas tree.*
HENRY: Karen, Judy, Ruth, come here! I got the most expensive
tree they had.

> (*The family is gathered round the tree, excited by their presents.*)

RUTH: What do you think, Mommy?
HENRY: Come here, Karen.
KAREN: I love her. I love them all.
RUTH: I love the gold outfit.
HENRY: Merry Christmas.
KAREN: Thank you. Merry Christmas.
HENRY: What? And? (*They kiss.*) And?
KAREN: Merry Christmas.
HENRY: Happy Hanukah.
KAREN: Very funny. Very funny.
HENRY: (*He gives her a wad of bills*) Go get yourself something
nice, okay?
KAREN: Okay.
HENRY: (*Voice-over*) Lufthansa should have been our ultimate
score. The heist of a lifetime. Six million in cash. More than
enough to go round.

INT. STACKS EDWARDS' APARTMENT. MORNING

STACKS EDWARDS *is in bed. His apartment is a mess.* TOMMY *and* CARBONE *are outside his door.*

TOMMY: Yo, Stacks!

STACKS EDWARDS: (*Waking up, coughing and sniffing*) Yeah, yeah, yeah. Hey, you guys. (*He lets them in.*)

TOMMY: What is it with you, huh? Oh, this fucking guy ain't ready. I knew you weren't going to be ready.

STACKS EDWARDS: Did you bring coffee?

TOMMY: What do I look like, a fucking caterer? Come on, Frankie will make coffee. Get up. Frankie, make coffee. Thought you'd have one of your bitches in here.

STACKS EDWARDS: Yeah, I did. Hey, where the fuck is she?

TOMMY: Always got these hot books around though or a bitch or something.

STACKS EDWARDS: What fucking time is it?

TOMMY: It's eleven thirty. We were supposed to be here. You know, we were supposed to be there by nine.

STACKS EDWARDS: Shit. I'll be ready in just a minute.

TOMMY: Yeah, you're always fucking late. You were late for your own fucking funeral.
(*As* STACKS EDWARDS *bends over for his shoes,* TOMMY *pulls out his gun and shoots him in the back of the head. Blood splatters the walls.* CARBONE *wanders in from the kitchen clasping a coffee pot.*)

TOMMY: What the fuck you looking at? Come on, make that coffee to go. Let's go.

CARBONE: *Come faccio. Iamunenne . . .*[1]

TOMMY: What the fuck you doing? It's a joke. A joke. Put the fucking pot down. You going to take the coffee?

CARBONE: *Va bene.*[2]

HENRY: (*Voice-over*) Stacks was always crazy. Instead of getting rid of the truck like he was supposed to do, he got stoned, went to his girlfriend's and by the time he woke the cops had found the truck. It was all over the television. They even said

---

1 Sicilian for 'How can I? Let's go.'
2 Sicilian for 'Okay.'

they came up with prints off the wheel. It was just a matter of
time before they got to Stacks.

INT. ROBERT'S LOUNGE. NIGHT

An agitated HENRY *walks into the bar and finds* JIMMY, TOMMY
and CARBONE *celebrating.*
TOMMY: How you doin'?
HENRY: (*To Jimmy*) I gotta talk to you.

TOMMY: Have a drink.

JIMMY: Have a drink. Come on, have a drink.

TOMMY: Give them all a drink.

JIMMY: Come on, have a drink. What are you doing?

HENRY: I gotta talk to you.

JIMMY: This is an occasion. Have a drink.

HENRY: I-I-I've still got to talk to you.

JIMMY: All right.

> (JIMMY *grabs* HENRY *round the neck and they go into the backroom.*)

JIMMY: What? What? What? What?

HENRY: What happened with Stacks? Is everything okay?

JIMMY: Naw, don't worry about that. It's all right.

HENRY: Jimmy, there's Feds all over the place.

JIMMY: Yeah, so what? Where are they gonna go? Where are they gonna go?

HENRY: It's – Uh, uh, in the papers.

> (TOMMY *joins them.*)

JIMMY: He's worried.

TOMMY: What are you, what are you worried about?

HENRY: No, just the, uh, the television and the newspapers. All this shit's out there.

JIMMY: What are you worried about?

TOMMY: You worry too much. The – (*Kissing* HENRY.) Everything is beautiful. There's nothing to worry about. Didn't you tell him?

JIMMY: Naw, I didn't tell him yet.

HENRY: What?

JIMMY: Guess what? They're gonna make him.

HENRY: Paulie's gonna make you?

JIMMY: Yeah.

HENRY: Tommy.

JIMMY: They opened up the books. Paulie got the okay. Can you believe that? This little guinea bastard. Can you believe that?

JIMMY: Huh? Huh? He's gonna get made. We're gonna work for this guy one day. He's gonna be boss.

HENRY: (*Chuckling*) Tommy!

JIMMY: I can't believe it.

HENRY: I'm happy for you. That's great. Congratulations.

TOMMY: Motherfuckers, we got 'em now.

(*At the door,* MORRIE *tries to speak to* JIMMY *again.* JIMMY *and* TOMMY *walk past him angrily, but* HENRY *is caught.*)

MORRIE: Hey Jimmy, I've been looking all over for you, baby. Jimmy, can I talk to you a second, hey?

HENRY: Morrie, Morrie, Morrie, don't.

MORRIE: Hen, what is it?

HENRY: Come on. Come on.

MORRIE: I masterminded the goddamn thing, I'm left with dick.

HENRY: Morrie.

MORRIE: They'd be up a creek without a paddle if not for me.

HENRY: Morrie, all right.

MORRIE: Fuck him! I want my money.

HENRY: Morrie.

MORRIE: Henry, I want my fucking money. I had it up to here.

HENRY: All right.

MORRIE: That cheap cigarette hijacking mick!

HENRY: Morrie! Shh.

MORRIE: No, fuck him! I want my money.

HENRY: Good. Go tell him (*He stands back.*) Now are you gonna keep your mouth shut or what? Huh? Morrie, you're gonna get your money. You just gotta stop busting balls. All right. Look at me. You hear me? Look – Look at me, okay? Everything's gonna be fine.

MORRIE: Henry.

HENRY: What?

MORRIE: (*Begins singing*)
'Oh, Henry, Boy,
The Pipes, the Pipes are Calling'

HENRY: Oh, Morrie.

MORRIE: Hey, sweetheart, half mick half guinea? I'll sing with an Italian accent. (*Singing*)
'And down through the Glen
Through the Glen, the Glen
And down the Mountainside'

HENRY: Just –

MORRIE: (*Singing*)
'Vo Vo Vo Vi'
(*Speaking*) You're a doll. Thanks, but on the other hand –

HENRY: (*Interrupting*) Don't.

MORRIE: You're right. When you're right, you're right.

(*Singing*)
> 'The Summer's Gone
> And All the Roses Dying'

(HENRY *leads* MORRIE *back to the bar.*)
> 'It's You, It's You
> And I must . . .'

(JIMMY *is seated at the bar, looking intently at* MORRIE.)

EXT. THE SIDEWALK OUTSIDE ROBERT'S LOUNGE BAR.
NEXT DAY

HENRY *and* JIMMY, *in an agitated state, are walking together.*

HENRY: (*Voice-over*) I could see for the first time that Jimmy
was a nervous wreck. His mind was going in eight different
directions at once.

JIMMY: Do you think Morrie tells his wife everything?

HENRY: Morrie? Him? (*The frame freezes.*)

HENRY: (*Voice-over*) That's when I knew Jimmy was gonna
whack Morrie. That's how it happens. That's how fast it
takes for a guy to get whacked. (*The movement continues.*)

HENRY: You know him. He's a nut job. He talks to everybody.
You see his commercials, acting like a jerk. Nobody listens
to what he says. Nobody fucking cares what he says, he
talks so much.

JIMMY: Make sure you bring him here tonight, hm? Okay?

HENRY: All right.

INT. ROBERT'S LOUNGE BAR. EVENING

The wiseguys are playing cards. Among them are HENRY, MORRIE,
CARBONE, TOMMY *and* JIMMY. *They are all joking and laughing
as normal.*

MORRIE: Start like this. (*He blows.*) Oh, sorry. Did I get you in
the eye?

CARBONE: Morrie, stop breaking my balls, all right?

HENRY: (*Voice-over*) I was just stalling for time. I knew I still
had till eight or nine o'clock to talk Jimmy out of killing

Morrie. But meanwhile as far as Jimmy knew, I was going along with the program.

TOMMY: You're laughing, but it was a funny situation. You don't know what to do. Thirty witnesses, right! I killed this motherfucker. I swear I killed him. I go back, I fucking beat his head in. Bang him against the fucking wall. I got him on the ground, pulling hair out of the fucking head. I bit him. He's out fucking cold.

HENRY: Come on, let's go! Let's go!

TOMMY: I'm fucking – I'm enraged. I want to kill this little fuck.

CARBONE: Yeah.

TOMMY: I walk away. We start to go in the fucking joint. All of a sudden I don't want to turn around. Jimmy's going like this to me. (*Laughter.*) I don't want to fuckin' turn around. I don't want to turn around. He picks up his fucking head, he says, 'Ah, ah, ah, jerkoff!'

MORRIE: Get out of here.

TOMMY: Jerkoff! What are you gonna do? What are you gonna do? Now I fuckin' fly at him. I got him out and I'm fuckin' banging his head. I'm banging his fuckin' head. I beat him to a pulp, to a pulp. To a fucking pulp, I got him. He's laying there full of fucking blood. I'm out of breath. I got blood all over my fucking clothes.

JIMMY: (*In* HENRY'*s ear*) Forget about tonight. Forget about tonight.

TOMMY: He's laughing at me all the while he's laughing, I don't want to look.

HENRY: (*Voice-over*) It was like a load off my mind. Poor bastard. He never knew how close he'd come to getting killed. Even if I told him he would have never believed me.

EXT. ROBERT'S LOUNGE. DAWN

JIMMY, TOMMY *and* CARBONE *are leaving the bar after a long night.* MORRIE *is still trying to get Jimmy's attention.*

MORRIE: Jimmy, could I talk to you now?

JIMMY: Son-of-a-bitch. You know you're a pisser.

MORRIE: Yeah.

JIMMY: You're a real pisser.
> (MORRIE *laughs*.)
> You want to talk now?
MORRIE: Please.
JIMMY: Okay, let's talk. Let's get it over with.
MORRIE: Okay.
JIMMY: I swear to God I've never known a ball buster like you in my whole life. (*He laughs*.)
MORRIE: Hey, who loves you more than I do, huh?
JIMMY: (*To* CARBONE) What do you think of this guy?
MORRIE: I'll do anything for you.
JIMMY: Yeah, except to stop busting my balls. (*Everyone laughs*.) Come on, let's go have coffee.
MORRIE: Oh, you want to go to a diner or what?
CARBONE: Well, we'll go to a diner over there on the Boulevard.
JIMMY: Yeah. Now which – which diner?
CARBONE: Uh, Rockaway Boulevard.
JIMMY: Oh, there.
CARBONE: It's open twenty-four hours so.
MORRIE: They got Danish there?
CARBONE: Yeah, they got everything.
MORRIE: Yeah, let's pick up some Danish for Belle. Take a couple home.
> (*They all get inside Carbone's car,* MORRIE *taking the front seat with* TOMMY *behind him*.)
CARBONE: Did you hear about the points were were shaving up in Boston?
MORRIE: No, I didn't hear.
CARBONE: Oh, It's terrific, yeah. Nunzio up inj–
> (TOMMY *pulls* MORRIE's *head back and thrusts an ice pick into his neck.* MORRIE *is soon dead.*)
TOMMY: I thought he'd never shut the fuck up.
JIMMY: What a pain in the ass.
TOMMY: What do you want to do with him?
JIMMY: Get rid of him. Chop him up and get rid of the car. Call me when you get through. (*He gets out of the car and walks off.*)
TOMMY: All right. All right, Frankie, let's chop him up.
CARBONE: (*About to get out of the car*) All right, let's go.

TOMMY: Where are you going? Where are you going, you dizzy motherfucker, you?

CARBONE: What? I thought you said to chop him up.

TOMMY: Come on. Up at Charlie's. Not here.

CARBONE: Charlie's?

TOMMY: Where the fuck we gonna chop him up here?

CARBONE: *Metto la luce, Dio cane.*[1]

TOMMY: Come on, what are you doing? Get the fuck outta here.

CARBONE: All right, let me think. All right. *Va bene. Va bene.*

TOMMY: I got a better shot letting him fuckin' drive. What are you waiting for?

CARBONE: I'm waiting – The car's cold. *Buttiglia diavolo. Minghia.* This fuckin' thing –

TOMMY: (*Interrupting*) Get the fuck outta here! What fuckin' warm it up? Get outta here!

CARBONE: *E calma.*[2]

INT. HENRY AND KAREN'S HOUSE. NIGHT

The doorbell rings, waking HENRY and KAREN from sleep.

HENRY: Who is it?

KAREN: It's Belle. It's Belle. Open up.

BELLE: It's Belle. Let me in. Oh, please. (*She is very distraught.*) Oh, Morris didn't come home. He's missing. I-I know something's happened.

HENRY: Belle. Belle, calm down.

KAREN: It's all right. Everything will be okay.

HENRY: What? What are you saying? Come on –

BELLE: (*Interrupting*) He's missing. I know something happened.

HENRY: Uh, he's probably drunk and fell asleep somewhere. I'll go looking for him in the morning, okay?

BELLE: In twenty-seven years he's never been away all night without calling. I know something's happened. I know, you know.

KAREN: No –

HENRY: Belle. Belle, let me, let me go upstairs and get changed.

[1] Sicilian for 'I'm putting on the lights, damn it.'
[2] Sicilian for 'Calm down.'

I'll take you home and then I'll go lookin' for him.
BELLE: Take me home? I've been home. I've been home. I've
been on the phone. I've been calling –
HENRY: (*To himself*) Oh, fuck!
KAREN: He's in a card game.

EXT. THE PARKING LOT OUTSIDE SHERWOOD DINER. DAWN

HENRY *and* JIMMY *are leaving together.*
HENRY: So what the fuck do you want me to tell Belle?
JIMMY: Well, who gives a fuck? Tell her – Tell her . . . Tell her
he ran off with some broad. What do you care about her?
(*He sees two* FBI *agents who have been tailing him asleep in their
car.*)
Watch this.
HENRY: Naw, don't fuck with them.
JIMMY: Ah, I do it all the time. I'll bust their fucking balls.
HENRY: Don't even give them the satisfaction, the fucks.
JIMMY: (*He raps on the window of the agents' car*) Come on,
fuckos. Let's go for a ride. (HENRY *laughs.* JIMMY *gets in his
car.*) Keep 'em up all night.
HENRY: All right. I'll see you later.
JIMMY: I'll see you later.

EXT. A STREET IN BROOKLYN. DAY

*Some kids walk over to peek in the pink Cadillac convertible that
belonged to* JOHNNY ROASTBEEF. *The camera cranes up to reveal his
slumped body alongside that of his* WIFE. *There is blood on their faces
from bullet wounds.*
HENRY: (*Voice-over*) Jimmy was cutting every link between
himself and the robbery, but it had nothing to do with me. I
gave Jimmy the tip and he gave me some Christmas money.

EXT. BEHIND THE AIRPORT DINER. DAWN

*A large garbage truck backs up to a dumpster. As it is tipped over, the
bodies of* FRENCHY *and* JOE BUDDHA *are discovered amongst the
garbage.*

GARBAGE MAN: Hold it, Pat! Hold it up, man.

HENRY: (*Voice-over*) From then on I kept my mouth shut. And I knew Jimmy. He had the cash. It was his. I know he kicked some money upstairs to Paulie, but that was it.

EXT. THE HUNTS POINT MARKET PARKING LOT. MORNING

The police have surrounded a large refrigeration truck. As the rear doors are opened, the camera moves inside to discover the frozen body of FRANKIE CARBONE.

HENRY: (*Voice-over*) It made him sick to have to turn money over to the guys who stole it. He'd rather whack 'em. Anyway, what did I care? I wasn't asking for anything and besides Jimmy was making nice money with me through my Pittsburgh connections. But still, months after the robbery they were finding bodies all over. When they found Carbone in the meat truck, he was frozen so stiff it took them two days to thaw him out for the autopsy.

INT. SHERWOOD DINER. DAY

On a sunny afternoon, HENRY *and* JIMMY *are seated in a window booth, eating breakfast.*

HENRY: So, do you want to call him again? I think you only called him about four times so far.

HENRY: (*Voice-over*) Still, I never saw Jimmy so happy.

JIMMY: No, give me a minute.

HENRY: Sure you don't want to call one more time?

JIMMY: No, I'll call him right away. I'll give him about a few more minutes to get home.

HENRY: What is it with you and the phone, huh? What is it with you and the phone?

JIMMY: I'm trying to call the guy. That's what he said last week. I'll tell you what a pisser, when this guy gets made.

HENRY: Can you imagine working for him?

HENRY: (*Voice-over*) He was like a kid. We had money coming in through my Pittsburgh people and even after a while the Lufthansa thing began to calm down. But the thing that made Jimmy so happy that morning was that this was the day

105

that Tommy was being made. Jimmy was so excited you'd think he was being made. He must have made four calls to Tommy's house. They had a signal all set up so he'd know that the minute the ceremony was over.

EXT. TOMMY'S MOTHER'S HOUSE. DAY

All dressed up, TOMMY *is preparing to leave for the ceremony.*

TOMMY: Ma? Ma, where are you?

TOMMY'S MOTHER: Oh, here I am.

TOMMY: Oh.

TOMMY'S MOTHER: You're home.

TOMMY: Home? I'm leaving. I've been here all the while.

TOMMY'S MOTHER: Yeah. That's right. You listen. Let me look at you. You look lovely.

TOMMY: What do you think? I look good, huh?

TOMMY'S MOTHER: You look wonderful. Listen.

TOMMY: Yeah?

TOMMY'S MOTHER: Just be careful. Congratulations. I wish you lots of luck.

TOMMY: I love you. Don't paint any more religious pictures, please.

TOMMY'S MOTHER: Okay. Be careful.

TOMMY: All right.

TOMMY'S MOTHER: God be with you.

TOMMY: 'Bye, Ma.

(TOMMY *walks out of the house to find* VINNIE *and* TUDDY *by a waiting car.*)

TUDDY: Hey, Tommy.

HENRY: (*Voice-over*) You know, we always called each other good fellas. Like you said to, uh, somebody, 'You're gonna like this guy. He's all right. He's a good fella. He's one of us.' You understand? We were good fellas. Wiseguys.

(*They drive off.*)

INT. SHERWOOD DINER

JIMMY *has just finished his breakfast.*

JIMMY: I better call him. (*He goes outside to a phone booth.*)

HENRY: (*Voice-over*) But Jimmy and I could never be made

because we had Irish blood. It didn't even matter that my mother was Sicilian. To become a member of a crew you've got to be one hundred per cent Italian so they can trace all your relatives back to the old country. See, it's the highest honor they can give you. It means you belong to a family and crew. It means that nobody can fuck around with you. It also means you could fuck around with anybody just as long as they aren't also a member. It's like a license to steal. It's a license to do anything.

INT. THE GARAGE OF A ONE-FAMILY BUILDING

The car with TOMMY *pulls into a basement garage.* TOMMY *is lead by* VINNIE *and* TUDDY *into an adjoining room.*

VINNIE: *Buona fortuna,*[1] Tommy

TOMMY: All right, thanks, Vinnie. Hey, how many years ago since you was made?

VINNIE: Nah, I'm an old timer. Thirty years ago.

TOMMY: Thirty years, huh?

VINNIE: Yep.

TOMMY: Brings back a lot of memories.

VINNIE: And how.

TOMMY: Pike's Peak was a fucking pimple then, wasn't it? (*They laugh.*)

HENRY: (*Voice-over*) As far as Jimmy was concerned with Tommy being made, it was like we were all being made. We would now have one of our own as a member.

TOMMY *proudly walks into the room. It is empty. He realizes what this means as he is shot in the back of the head.*

TOMMY: Oh no!

EXT. THE PHONE BOOTH BY SHERWOOD DINER

JIMMY *is speaking to* VINNIE *on the phone.*

JIMMY: Yeah.

VINNIE: (*Over telephone*) Yeah.

JIMMY: Who's this?

[1] Sicilian for 'Good luck.'

VINNIE: This is Vinnie, Jim.

JIMMY: Vinnie, what's happened?

VINNIE: Well, we had a –

JIMMY: (*Interrupting*) Everything get straightened out?

VINNIE: Well, we had a problem. And, uh, we tried to do everything we could.

JIMMY: What do you mean?

VINNIE: Well, you know what I mean. He's gone. And we couldn't do nothing about it. That's it.

JIMMY: What do you mean? What do you mean? Uh . . .

VINNIE: He's gone. Uh, he's gone. And that's it.

(*Crying with anger and frustration,* JIMMY *slams down the phone.*)

JIMMY: Motherfucker! Mother . . . I knew it! I can't fucking believe it. I can't fucking believe – I can't fucking – What the fuck –

HENRY: What happened?

JIMMY: They whacked him. They fucking whacked him. (*He kicks over the phone booth.*)

HENRY: Oh, fuck.

JIMMY: Mother– Motherfuck. (*Sobbing.*) Motherfucker!

HENRY: Are you all right?

INT. THE BASEMENT ROOM OFF THE GARAGE

VINNIE *and* TUDDY *stand over Tommy's body. Blood flows from his head.*

HENRY: (*Voice-over*) It was revenge for Billy Batts, and a lot of things.

VINNIE: And that's that.

HENRY: (*Voice-over*) And there was nothing we could do about it. Batts was a made man and Tommy wasn't. And we had to sit still and take it. It was among the Italians. It was real greaseball shit. They even shot Tommy in the face so his mother couldn't give him an open coffin at the funeral.

EXT. HENRY'S DRIVEWAY. DAY

Sunday 11 May 1980 6:55 a.m.

After snorting cocaine, HENRY *leaves his house and puts a paper bag*

filled with guns into the trunk of his car. He hears the noise of a
helicopter, then sees it in the sky. He slams the trunk closed, and drives
off to meet JIMMY. *Events move at a very fast pace.*

HENRY: (*Voice-over*) I was gonna be busy all day. I had to drop off
some guns at Jimmy's to match some silencers he had gotten. I
had to pick up my brother at the hospital and drive him back
to the house for dinner that night, and then I had to pick up
some new Pittsburgh stuff for Lois to fly down to some
customers I had near Atlanta.

EXT. JIMMY'S DOORWAY

JIMMY *tries unsuccessfully to screw his silencers on to Henry's guns.*
They don't fit, and JIMMY *is running our of patience.*

JIMMY: What did I tell ya? Yeah, none of these fucking things fit, I
can't . . . Hey, hey, hey.

HENRY: (*Voice-over*) Right away I knew he didn't want them. I knew
I was going to get stuck for the money. I only bought the damn
guns because he wanted them and now he didn't want them.

JIMMY: They don't work. Hey, what the fuck good are these
things? None of them fit. What's the matter with you? What
are we – What do you want me to pay for this shit? I'm not
paying for it.

HENRY: (*Voice-over*) I didn't say a thing. Jimmy was so pissed off
he didn't even say good-bye.

JIMMY: And stop with the fucking drugs. They're making your
mind into mush. You hear me?

HENRY: All right. I'll take 'em back.
(HENRY *puts the torn bag with the guns back into the car trunk.*)

EXT. HENRY'S CAR. DAY

8:05 a.m.

HENRY *is speeding along the highway approaching Queens Midtown*
Tunnel.

INT. HENRY'S CAR

HENRY: (*Voice-over*) I knew my Pittsburgh guys always wanted guns and since I was gonna see them later in the afternoon to pick up delivery, I was pretty sure I'd get my money back. (HENRY *looks up and sees the helicopter again. When he looks back at the road he is suddenly confronted by a traffic jam ahead caused by an accident. He jams his foot on the brakes just in time.*)

INT. HOSPITAL ROOM. DAY

8:45 a.m.

A bedraggled HENRY *finds his brother* MICHAEL *dressed and waiting in his wheelchair for him. Michael's* DOCTOR *is concerned about* HENRY's *state.*

HENRY: (*Voice-over*) When I finally got there at the hospital to pick up Michael, his doctor wanted to put me to bed.

HENRY: Michael, how you doing? You ready?

MICHAEL: Henry, the horse . . .

HENRY: (*Interrupting*) Sorry I'm late. How you doing, Doc?

DOCTOR: Hey, wait a minute. Wait a minute. Jesus Christ, what happened to you?

HENRY: Well, uh, noth– I just almost got into an accident right now, driving over here. And I've been partying all night. I'm okay.

DOCTOR: Well now, come over here and let me check you out, huh?

HENRY: (*Voice-over*) I told him about the accident and I said I was partying all night.

HENRY: No, I'm fine, Doc.

DOCTOR: Come on, get over here.

HENRY: Doc, I'm fine.

DOCTOR: Let me check you out. Come on.

HENRY: (*Voice-over*) Well, he took mercy on me. He gave me ten milligrams of Valium and sent me home.
    (HENRY *is wheeling* MICHAEL *down the corridor of the hospital. He sees the helicopter again.*)

MICHAEL: All right

HENRY: I really had a close call. Listen, I got to get you home right away, 'cause I got a bunch of stuff I got to do.

HENRY: (*Voice-over*) Now my plan was to drop off my brother at the house, and pick up Karen.

HENRY: Just stuff I gotta do. I gotta make a –

INT. HENRY'S CAR. DAY

HENRY *is driving* MICHAEL *home*.

HENRY: There it is. You see that, Michael? You see that
    helicopter? You see it right there?

MICHAEL: Where?

HENRY: Right in front of us there.

MICHAEL: Yeah, yeah.

HENRY: I think it's been following me all morning.

MICHAEL: Get the fuck outta here. What are you, nuts?

HENRY: I'm telling ya. I don't know what's going on. It's the
    third time I've seen it. I-I-I went to the hospital. I started out
    to get you. I had to stop somewhere. Make some couple stops.

MICHAEL: What, are you fucking . . .

HENRY: I've seen it every time. I've been all over town and the
    thing, I've seen it all day. See?

INT. HENRY'S KITCHEN. DAY

11.30 a.m.

HENRY *is making meatballs.* MICHAEL, *in his wheelchair, is preparing
vegetables with* KAREN *and* LOIS. *The children are trying to help.*

HENRY: Michael, make sure you cut those thin.

MICHAEL: Thin, yeah.

HENRY: You too. Judy and Ruth. All right?

JUDY: Okay.

HENRY: (*Voice-over*) You see I was cooking dinner that night and
    I had to start braising the beef, pork butt and veal shanks for
    the tomato sauce.

MICHAEL: Are you using canned tomatoes?

HENRY: Karen . . . No. I'm gonna make the b– I'm going to make
    'em all. I'm going to make all this meat . . . I'm gonna make
    all the meatballs here. I have about twenty . . . twenty-four.
    I'll get twenty-four out of this. Here, easy, easy, easy.

HENRY: (*Voice-over*) It was Michael's favorite. I was making ziti
    with the meat gravy and I'm planning to roast some peppers

over the flames and I was gonna put on some string beans with some olive oil and garlic, and I had some beautiful cutlets that were cut just right, that I was going to fry up before dinner just as an appetizer. So I was home for about an hour. Now my plan was to start the dinner early so Karen and I could unload the guns that Jimmy didn't want, and then get the package for Lois to take to Atlanta for her trip later that night.

MICHAEL: Who's been carving their initials in the tomato?

HENRY: (*Voice-over*) Now I kept looking out the window and I saw that the helicopter was gone.

MICHAEL: Henry.

HENRY: Karen? Michael, keep an eye on the sauce, all right? (*To the children.*) You stay here with your Uncle Michael, all right? I'll see you later.

JUDY: All right.

HENRY: (*Voice-over*) So I asked my brother Michael to watch the sauce and Karen and I started out.

KAREN: I'll call you if it's more than a couple of hours, all right?

JUDY: 'Bye.

INT. HENRY'S CAR. DAY

HENRY *and* KAREN *are in the car.* KAREN *points out the helicopter.*

KAREN: Oh, God. Oh, God, I see it.

HENRY: What?

KAREN: I see it. Look, look, it's right there.

HENRY: Is she up? Damn! Yep, that's it.

KAREN: There it is, Henry. I see it.

HENRY: Come on, we gotta get – We gotta get to your mother's. See? I told ya.

KAREN: It's funny. Okay. It's funny. It's not the end of the world.

HENRY: Just – We're going to your mother's.

EXT. KAREN'S MOTHER'S GARAGE AREA. DAY

Once out of the car, HENRY *puts the guns into garbage cans.*

HENRY: Karen. Go inside and tell your mother not to touch anything outside the house. Nothing, all right?

KAREN: You couldn't have gone to your mother's house. You had to come here.

(*The helicopter still seems to be following them.*)

HENRY: Come on. Let's go shopping. Come on.

EXT. A LONG ISLAND SHOPPING MALL. DAY

12:30 p.m.

HENRY *is on the phone.*

HENRY: No, I'm not nuts. This thing's been following me around all fucking morning. I'm telling ya. Fine, fine. (*He hangs up and turns to* KAREN.) He thinks I'm paranoid. I should bring him the fucking helicopter, then we'll see how paranoid I am. Come on. Let's go inside.

EXT. SHOPPING MALL ENTRANCE. DAY

1:30 p.m.

HENRY *and* KAREN *leave the mall and search the sky for the helicopter. It is gone.*

HENRY: Yeah, it's gone.

KAREN: I don't hear anything.

HENRY: Come on, let's go back to your mother's.

EXT. KAREN'S MOTHER'S GARAGE AREA. DAY

HENRY *retrieves the guns from the garbage cans.*

INT. A MOTEL APARTMENT. DAY

3:30 p.m.

The DEALER *from Pittsburgh laughs as* HENRY *gives him the guns.*

HENRY: They all right?

DEALER: Beautiful. Beautiful. They're great. Great. Now, didn't I tell you you were paranoid? Karen, didn't I tell him he was paranoid?

KAREN: Yeah. I need a hit.

(*The* DEALER *takes* KAREN *aside to snort cocaine.*)

DEALER: (*He makes a whirring sound*) You want to see helicopters? Come on, I'll show you helicopters.

KAREN: No, that's all right.

DEALER: Come on.

KAREN: No, that's all right. I've seen enough helicopters for one day. Thank you.

DEALER: I'll show you helicopters.

HENRY: (*Voice-over*) My plan was I had to get home and get the package ready for Lois to take on her trip. Also, I had to get to Sandy's house to give the package a whack with quinine.
(*The* DEALER *hands over the heroin to* HENRY.)

DEALER: Look at this. One.

HENRY: Is this the same stuff?

DEALER: Yeah. Two . . . three . . . yeah.

HENRY: From the same guy?

DEALER: Four . . .

HENRY: Just four, just four.

HENRY: (*Voice-over*) Plus I knew Sandy was gonna get on my ass. Then I had the cooking to finish at home, and I had to get Lois ready for her trip.
(*The phone rings. The* DEALER *answers.*)

DEALER: Hello?

SANDY: (*Over telephone*) Henry?

DEALER: Hang on, I'll get him. (*To* HENRY.) It's Sandy. What the fuck is this?

HENRY: (*Whispering*) She's such a pain in the ass. (*Into telephone.*) Yeah.

DEALER: The fuckin' bitch always calls . . .

SANDY: Hey, Hen. When you coming over?

HENRY: I'll be there in about an hour.

SANDY: You're staying tonight, right?

HENRY: No, I can't, I can't. I got my brother tonight.

SANDY: Oh, Henry!

HENRY: Come on, stop, stop, stop. We'll talk about it later, okay?

SANDY: Yeah, whatever! 'Bye.

HENRY: Good-bye. (*To* DEALER.) Unbelievable.

INT. HENRY'S KITCHEN. DAY

MICHAEL *is stirring the tomato sauce. The phone rings.* LOIS *answers it.*
LOIS: Hello.
HENRY: (*Over telephone*) Hey, it's me. Are you ready?
LOIS: Yeah.

INT. THE MOTEL APARTMENT

HENRY *is on the telephone to* LOIS.
HENRY: Listen, tell Michael not to let the sauce stick, to keep
    stirring it.

INT. HENRY'S KITCHEN

LOIS, *on the phone, turns to* MICHAEL.
LOIS: Henry says don't let the sauce stick.
MICHAEL: I'm stirring it.
HENRY: (*Over telephone*) Uh, listen, you know what to do?
LOIS: Yeah. Yeah.

INT. THE MOTEL APARTMENT

HENRY: (*Agitated, into telephone*) Don't yeah, yeah, me, Lois. This
    is important. Now make sure you leave the house when you
    make the call. You understand me? You hear me? Call from an
    outside line. I mean it.

INT. HENRY'S KITCHEN

LOIS: (*Into telephone*) Jesus, you must think I'm dumb. What are
    you bugging me for? I know what to do.
HENRY: (*Over telephone*) Hey, you . . .

INT. THE MOTEL APARTMENT

HENRY: (*Into telephone*) little hick, just make sure you do it. I mean
    what –
LOIS: (*Over telephone*) You can be such a pain.

INT. HENRY'S KITCHEN

HENRY: (*Over telephone*) Hey! Just do it!
LOIS: (*Into telephone*) Okay. (*She hangs up.*)

INT. THE MOTEL APARTMENT

HENRY *hangs up.*
HENRY: Unfucking believable. All of 'em. Every fucking girl in my
    life.

INT. HENRY'S KITCHEN

MICHAEL: What did he say?
LOIS: Nothing.
    (LOIS *takes an airline ticket out of her bag. Freeze frame.*)
HENRY: (*Voice-over*) So what does she do after she hangs up with
    me? After everything I told her. After all her yeah, yeah, yeah,
    bullshit, she picks up the phone and calls from the house.
    Now if anybody was listening they'd know everything.
    They'd know that a package was leaving from my house, and
    they'd even have the time and the flight number thanks to her.
    (LOIS *reaches for the kitchen phone and dials.*)
LOIS: Hi, it's Lois.

INT. HENRY'S KITCHEN. EVENING

6:30 p.m.

HENRY *is back working in the kitchen with his family and* LOIS.
JUDY: Lois.
LOIS: Yeah?
JUDY: What's a zombie?
LOIS: I told you what a zombie is before. Don't you remember
    what I said last night? A zombie is a dead person who comes
    back to life.
KAREN: What are you reading?
HENRY: (*Voice-over*) As soon as I got home I started cooking. I had
    a few hours until Lois's flight. I told my brother to keep an eye
    on the stove.

116

HENRY: All right, Michael. Michael. Keep an eye on the sauce
    and watch out for helicopters, and don't let Karen touch the
    sauce.
HENRY: (*Voice-over*) All day long the poor guy's been watching
    helicopters and tomato sauce. You see I had to drive over to
    Sandy's place, mix the stuff once and then get back to the gravy.
MICHAEL: I'll guard it with my life.

INT. SANDY'S APARTMENT. EVENING

8:30 p.m.

SANDY *mixes the heroin. The table is still a mess of mixing bowls,
scales and sieves.* HENRY *takes a snort of cocaine.*
SANDY: (*Looking in bad shape*) What do you think you can come
    over here and fuck me and leave? Huh?
HENRY: Come on.
SANDY: You got some better place to go, huh?
HENRY: Don't talk like that. Come on. You all right?
SANDY: Yeah, sure.
HENRY: Do you believe me? Huh? Do you believe me? Do you
    believe me? (*They kiss.*) Is that the last one?
SANDY: Yeah.
HENRY: Oh. (*He laughs mockingly as he bolts out of the door.*)
SANDY: You fuckin' lying son-of-a-bitch, I hate you!

INT. HENRY'S DINING ROOM. NIGHT

10:45 p.m.

The Hill family are finishing their dinner. HENRY *looks exhausted.*
LOIS: (*To the children*) Take off your crust, right? Dip it in a little
    water or your soda there, and then you – woops – and then
    you start to sort of mold it into the natural play-dough.
KAREN: (*To* JUDY) Please stop feeding the dog from the table,
    from the plate on top of it. Stop it.
JUDY: I have to.
KAREN: You don't have to.
MICHAEL: Remember the family here?
KAREN: My problem is the dog will constantly yap!

(HENRY *and* LOIS *move into the kitchen.*)

LOIS: I gotta go home.

HENRY: What do you mean you gotta go home? I've been carrying around this stuff all day. We gotta start taping it to your leg. We got to go soon.

LOIS: I gotta go home and get my hat.

HENRY: Forget your fucking hat. What are you kidding me? Just what I need now is a trip to Rockaway because you want to get your hat?

LOIS: I need it. I gotta have it. It's my lucky hat. I never fly without it.

HENRY: Lois, do you understand what we're involved in here?

LOIS: I don't care. I need my hat. I won't fly without it.

HENRY: Fuck!

HENRY: (*Voice-over*) What could I do? If she insisted I had to drive her home for her goddamn hat. I threw the package in the kitchen and I went to take her home.

(HENRY *hides the heroin in a kitchen cupboard.*)

HENRY: Karen! The stuff's in here. I gotta take her to get her fucking hat.

KAREN: A hat?

EXT. HENRY'S DRIVEWAY. NIGHT

HENRY *and* LOIS *get in his car.*

LOIS: Just relax, will you!

HENRY: For a hat I got to do this bullshit.

(*Moving out of the driveway,* HENRY *notices there are cars and lights flashing everywhere. Suddenly, a* NARC *appears at his window and jams a gun against Henry's head.*)

HENRY: What the fuck is this?

NARC: Police! Freeze! Don't you move, you motherfucker. I'll blow your brains out. Shut the car off slowly.

HENRY: (*Voice-over*) For a second I thought I was dead, but when I heard all the noise I knew they were cops. Only cops talk that way. If they had been wiseguys, I wouldn't have heard a thing. I would've been dead.

NARC: Don't move.

INT. HENRY AND KAREN'S HOUSE. NIGHT

KAREN *is thrown into panic. The* COPS *are at the front door.*

KAREN: Michael, lock the door!

COP: Open up, it's the police!

KAREN: Michael!

COP: Open up! Open up! It's the police! Open up! Open up!

    (KAREN *hurriedly flushes the heroin down the toilet upstairs.*)

COP: It's the police! Open up! Open up! Open up! Open up!

KAREN: Okay. Okay.

    (KAREN *goes to the bureau drawer, takes out a small calibre gun,*
    and shoves it into her underpants.)

COP: It's the police! Open up! We're coming in! We're coming in!
    Open up!

INT. FBI OFFICE

The Aftermath

HENRY *is seated and surrounded by* NARC OFFICERS.

FIRST NARC: Here, talk. Talk to me. Talk to me. When was the
    last time you took a collar? Hey, fuckhead, I'm talking to
    you!

SECOND NARC: It's beautiful.

FIRST NARC: You don't want to say a word to me, you don't have
    to say anything to me. I don't really give a fuck! Twenty-five
    years, pal, that's what you're gonna do. And see how much
    of a good guy you're gonna be then. All your pals are locked
    up, pal.

    (LOIS *is brought in.*)

HENRY: (*Voice-over*) All day I thought the guys in the helicopters
    were just local cops busting my balls over Lufthansa. But
    they turned out to be Narcs.

FIRST NARC: I'm just gonna ask you a couple of questions.

HENRY: Just get the fucking lawyer.

FIRST NARC: All right.

HENRY: (*Voice-over*) They'd been on me a month. Phone taps.
    Surveillance. Everything.

    (*The* DEALER *is hauled in past* HENRY.)

DEALER: All right. Come on. I can get here, Jesus.

FIRST NARC: You know the boys. How you doing, boys? All the pals are here. You don't want to talk to me, you're gonna have a fucking problem all night. I'm gonna be on you like shit. Each one of these counts holds twenty-five-to-life. Twenty-five-to-life felonies in New York State. How long you living on Long Island there? Twenty-five fucking years, pal. I'll slap your fucking head inside-out.

(SANDY *is brought in past* HENRY, *followed by boxes holding the pots, scales and sieves she used for mixing drugs.*)

SANDY: What the fuck is your problem! Get the fuck . . .

FIRST NARC: Jerry, what were you guys, grocery shopping? What are we gonna make, a cake? You're gonna make a fucking cake, too? You got anything good in there or what, Jerry? I-I-Is it good?

(*One of the* NARCS *licks his finger after wiping one of the bowls, and smiles.*)

FIRST NARC: 'Bye, 'bye, dickhead. (*Laughs.*) See you in Attica, dick.

INT. A PRISON VISITING AREA

KAREN *is sitting at a table facing* HENRY. *They try to avoid being heard by the* GUARDS.

KAREN: I spoke to Jimmy. He offered to give me some money. He just wants to know what's happening. He just wants to talk to you.

HENRY: Well, fuck Jimmy and his money. I told you I got to get out of here and straighten everything with Paulie or else I'm dead, Karen.

KAREN: Then you're better off staying in here.

HENRY: Karen, they could whack me in here just as easy as they could outside. Maybe even easier. They're all afraid I'm gonna rat them out. People are already walking away from me. I'm dead in here. You got to get me out.

HENRY: (*Voice-over*) Karen finally got her mother to put her house up for my bail and I was out. I remember I had this feeling I was gonna get killed right outside the jail. I knew Paulie was still pissed at me and he's such a hot head. And I was also worried about Jimmy. See, Jimmy knew if Paulie

found out he was in the drug deals with me, Paulie would have
Jimmy whacked even before me.

EXT. THE PRISON BAIL RELEASE GATE. NIGHT

HENRY *nervously leaves the prison.* KAREN *and* KAREN'S MOM *are
waiting in a car for him.*
KAREN'S MOM: Now what? What are they doing?
KAREN: You go on a diet for him?
KAREN'S MOM: Put your – Put your glasses on.
KAREN: Okay, okay, open the door.
    (HENRY *gets in the car.*)
KAREN'S MOM: He doesn't even say 'please'.
KAREN: Shh, Ma.
HENRY: (*Voice-over*) This is the bad time. I didn't feel safe until I
got home.

INT. THE BEDROOM IN HENRY AND KAREN'S HOUSE. NIGHT

HENRY *frantically looks around the bedroom.*
HENRY: Karen? Karen? Karen, where's the –
HENRY: (*Voice-over*) So now my plan was to stay alive long enough
    to sell off the dope that the cops never found and then
    disappear for a while until I can get things straightened out.
HENRY: W-Where the fuck is that. Karen! Fuck! Where's the stuff
    that I left? Karen?
KAREN: I flushed it down the toilet.
HENRY: You what?
KAREN: What was I supposed to do? They were all over the house.
HENRY: (*Yelling in anger*) Karen, that was worth sixty thousand
    dollars. I need that money! That's all we got!
KAREN: What was I supposed to do? They had a search warrant!
    They were in everything.
HENRY: Karen! That's all the money that we had, Karen! I was
    depending on that! Why did you do that?!
KAREN: I had to, really! They were gonna find it!
HENRY: Karen, what – Oh, fuck, Karen! They would never have
    found it!
KAREN: They would've found it! I swear to you, Henry! I swear,

Henry! They would've found it! (*Screaming*) Ohh, no!

HENRY: (*Yelling*) Why?!

KAREN: (*Crying*) They would've found it! I swear to you!

HENRY: Why did you do that, Karen?

KAREN: I had to do it, Henry.

HENRY: Oh, my God!

KAREN: I had to do it.

HENRY: Oh, my God!

(*They collapse together in the corner of the room.*)

Oh, God.

KAREN: Henry! No! No-o-o!

HENRY: Karen.

KAREN: (*Crying*) Ohh! Oh, God! Oh, God! Oh, no.

(*They lie on the bed asleep, a gun in* HENRY's *hand.*)

INT. GEFFKEN'S BAR. DAY

PAULIE *is in the kitchen cooking sausages. Several* HOODS *are in attendance.* HENRY *talks awkwardly to* PAULIE.

HENRY: Paulie, I'm really very sorry. I don't know what else to say. I know, I fucked up.

PAULIE: Fucked up. Yeah, you fucked up.

HENRY: You know but, I'm all right now. You know, I can be trusted now, Paulie. I'm clean. On my kids, I'm clean.

PAULIE: You looked in my eyes, you lied to me. You treated me like a fucking jerk. Like I was never nothing to you.

HENRY: Paulie, after what you said, I couldn't come to you. You know, I-I was, I was ashamed. But I got nowhere else to go, Paulie. You're all I've got. And I really, really need your help. I really do.

PAULIE: Take this.

(*Without counting it, he takes a wad of bills from his pocket and gives it to* HENRY.)

And now I got to turn my back on you.

HENRY: (*Crying*) Okay.

HENRY: (*Voice-over*) Thirty-two hundred bucks. That's what he gave me. Thirty-two hundred bucks for a lifetime. It wasn't even enough to pay for the coffin.

INT. THE BEDROOM IN HENRY AND KAREN'S HOUSE. NIGHT

HENRY *and* KAREN *try to make plans.*

HENRY: We got to get out!

KAREN: I don't wanna run. I don't want to – What am I supposed
to do, just pick up and leave everything? Go hiding? I don't
want to do that, Henry. Is that what you want?

HENRY: Karen, if we stay around here we're dead. You got it?
We're dead.

KAREN: They're right. You took too much of that stuff. You're
totally paranoid.

EXT. JIMMY'S JUKEBOX STOREFRONT. DAY

KAREN *is visiting* JIMMY *at his store.*

JIMMY: Oh, good. Thank you. How's he doing? Are they busting
his balls or what?

KAREN: He's okay.

JIMMY: Good.

KAREN: They sobered him up.

JIMMY: Good. Good. Good. Good. Very good. Glad to hear it.
You know what kind of questions they been asking him? Did
he tell you?

KAREN: Jimmy, I don't know. Huh. I mean, I got my mind on so
many other things. They – The girls are old enough to read
the newspapers.

JIMMY: Tell him he's got to call me, okay? As soon as you talk to
him, he's got to call me. We got to work on this whole thing.
It's very important.

KAREN: He doesn't know I came down here to see you. You
know, it's like he's crazy.

JIMMY: Take this for now. It's a couple thousand.

KAREN: Thanks, Jimmy.

JIMMY: Okay? Don't worry, honey. Everything's gonna be all
right. (*He kisses her.*) Listen, I got some beautiful Dior
dresses. You want to have 'em. Pick out a few for yourself.
Huh?

KAREN: For my mom?

JIMMY: Okay? Yeah, whatever. Take some.

KAREN: Yeah. Good. For my mom. (*She begins to climb a staircase.*)

JIMMY: No, no, no, no. It's over here. Great. It's in the store on the corner. It's swag so I got down the corner. Okay? All right, sweetheart. I'll see you. All right?
(*They walk out on to the sidewalk.*)

KAREN: Thank you, Jimmy.

JIMMY: Don't worry. Don't worry.

KAREN: I'll try.

JIMMY: All right. Don't forget. You got to call me.

KAREN: All right. Over there?

JIMMY: Right down there. Yeah.
(JIMMY *points* KAREN *to continue down the block past a series of empty storefronts.* KAREN *walks very hesitantly.*)

JIMMY: No, no. It's right over there. Right on the corner.
(KAREN *still walks very cautiously, looking back at* JIMMY.)
Yeah, it's over there. Right there.
(KAREN *can just make out some* CRATE LIFTERS *at work.*)

FIRST CRATE LIFTER: Take a look.

SECOND CRATE LIFTER: Shhh.

JIMMY: (*Calling out to* KAREN) No. No, no, no, no. Hey, go ahead! It's right in there!
(KAREN *hesitates, then quickly changes her mind and returns to her car.*)

KAREN: No, Jimmy! I'm in a hurry.

JIMMY: Right there.

KAREN: My mom's watching the kids. I got to get home.

JIMMY: Get the – It's right in the store.

KAREN: I'll come back later. (*She drives off.*)

EXT. THE DRIVEWAY OF HENRY AND KAREN'S HOUSE. DAY

KAREN, *visibly shaken by her experience, drives her car up to the garage. As it screeches to a halt,* HENRY *runs out, a gun at hand.*

HENRY: Karen? Karen? What happened? Karen?

KAREN: (*Crying*) Nothing.

HENRY: What happened?

KAREN: I just got scared.

HENRY: Okay.

KAREN: I just got scared.

HENRY: Got the keys?
KAREN: I got – I –
HENRY: What happened, Karen?
KAREN: I just got scared, Henry. It's o– It's okay.
HENRY: You all right?
KAREN: (*Sniffling*) Yeah.
HENRY: Shh.

INT. SHERWOOD DINER. LATE MORNING
HENRY *walks in and finds* JIMMY *at the window booth. Although there is food on the table, nothing seems to have been touched.*
HENRY: (*Voice-over*) If you're part of a crew, nobody ever tells you that they're going to kill you. It doesn't happen that way. There aren't any arguments or curses like in the movies. So your murderers come with smiles. They come as your friends, the people who have cared for you all your life, and they always seem to come at a time when you're at your weakest and most in need of their help. So I met Jimmy in a crowded place we both knew. I got there fifteen minutes early and I saw that Jimmy was already there.
JIMMY: Hey. Hi. How you doing?
HENRY: (*Voice-over*) He took the booth near the window so he could see everyone who drove up to the restaurant. He wanted to make sure I wasn't tailed. He was jumpy. He hadn't touched a thing.
HENRY: I'm just a little fucked up, but I'm, you know, I'll be okay.
JIMMY: You want something to eat?
HENRY: Naw, my stom–
JIMMY: Eat something.
HENRY: Naw, the aggravation's got my stomach going. I'm just gonna get a cup of coffee. That's it.
JIMMY: (*To* WAITRESS) Could we have a cup of coffee, please?
HENRY: (*Voice-over*) On the surface, of course, everything was supposed to be fine. We were supposed to be discussing my case. But I had the feeling Jimmy was trying to sense whether I was going to rat him out to save my neck.
JIMMY: You made sure nobody tailed you, didn't you?
HENRY: Oh, yeah. Yeah, you know, drove around for about half

an hour before I got here. In and out. So it's all right.

JIMMY: I been telling you all your whole life, don't talk on the fucking phone, right? Now you understand, huh? But it's gonna be okay. I think you got a good chance of beating the case. Yeah, well . . . You know that kid, you know, from the city we're talking about? You know I'm talking –

HENRY: Ye-eah . . .

JIMMY: Well, the kid turned out to be a rat. As soon as he got pinched, he ratted everybody out, he ratted youse all out. But I know where he is. He's hiding now. He's, you know, he's – Know what I'm saying? Would you have a problem going with Anthony on vacation? You know, take care of that?

HENRY: Uh-huh. No, not at all.

JIMMY: That way they got nothing. Huh?

(JIMMY *slips a matchbook across the table to* HENRY. *Freeze frames on* JIMMY *and then* HENRY.)

HENRY: (*Voice-over*) Jimmy had never asked me to whack somebody before. But now he's asking me to go down to

126

Florida and do a hit with Anthony. That's when I knew I
would never have come back from Florida alive.

JIMMY: Thank you.

HENRY: You know, um, I think I'll have another coffee.

WAITRESS: Yes, sure.

INT. AN FBI OFFICE. DAY

HENRY *and* KAREN *are being interviewed by* EDWARD MCDONALD.

HENRY: And do, do, you meant, wherever you move me, I asked
you once and I'm gonna tell you again, I don't want to go any
place that's cold.

EDWARD MCDONALD: You really don't have a choice in that
matter.

HENRY: Ed, come on. Just whoever fucking controls it, just no
place cold. All right? Do that for me. I'm trying to – I'm
doing, you know . . .

KAREN: He's bronchial, that's why.

EDWARD MCDONALD: Well, if he's legitimately bronchial we'll
take that into consideration.

HENRY: I'm legitimately bronchial. I would like to go someplace
that's not cold. If you could do that, great.

KAREN: Okay, can I, can I ask you s-some questions here? What
about my parents?

EDWARD MCDONALD: What about them?

KAREN: Am I gonna see them? Am I gonna talk to them? I mean,
w-w-wha- Don't I have some kind of contact with them?

EDWARD MCDONALD: No.

KAREN: No.

EDWARD MCDONALD: Well, that doesn't mean, uh –

KAREN: No. Wait a minute. Wait a minute. You mean to tell me
that God forbid something happens to my parents and they
get sick, I can't go and see them?

EDWARD MCDONALD: Maybe something can be worked out. If
they're sick. If there's some extraordinary set of
circumstances, maybe something can be worked out.

KAREN: I can't do this. I can't do this, Henry, I can't. (*Crying*.) I
can't leave my parents.

HENRY: Excuse me, Karen, I told you before, if you, uh – I'm not
going to do this unless you and the kids come with me. I-I

can't do it without you, okay? So you do whatever, but . . . that's it.

KAREN: You need Henry, but you don't need me, right?

EDWARD MCDONALD: That's right. And frankly, I don't care whether you go or not. If it's gonna make him a happier witness, a better witness, I'd like you to be with him.

KAREN: They want Henry, they don't want me.

EDWARD MCDONALD: But Henry's gonna be in the Witness Protection Program. They're not gonna be able to get to him. The only way they can get to him is by getting to you. Or getting to your kids. If he goes into the program, forget about it. You're in a great deal of danger. I think you understand that.

KAREN: I-I don't know anything.

EDWARD MCDONALD: Come on you don't know anything. Don't give me the babe-in-the-woods routine, Karen. I've listened to those wiretaps. And I've heard you on the telephone. You're talking about cocaine. Conversation after conversation you're talking to Henry on the phone. You're facing a lengthy prison sentence.

EXT. JUKEBOX STOREFRONT. DAY

JIMMY *is arrested by the* FBI.

INT. THE FBI OFFICE

EDWARD MCDONALD: It doesn't matter. Because whether he goes to jail, or whether he stays on the street and he beats the case, he's a dead man. He knows it and you know it.

HENRY: What about the kids? With school, what happens with them?

KAREN: Do they get left back? I mean, what goes on?

EDWARD MCDONALD: Why would they get left back? They'll just go to another community.

HENRY: I'm just asking you what happens.

INT. GEFFKEN'S BAR. DAY

PAULIE *is arrested by* FBI *agents*.

TUDDY: Hey . . . Why don't you guys go down to Wall Street and get some real fucking crooks. Whoever sold you those suits had a wonderful sense of humor.

GUYS AT BAR: Where do you guys think you're goin'? Get the fuck out'a here. You're a bunch of freeholes. You got nothin' better to do?

INT. THE FBI OFFICE

EDWARD MCDONALD: What it comes down to, Karen, is we're basically your only salvation. We're gonna save your life. We're gonna save his life. And we're gonna keep you out of jail.

INT. COURTROOM. DAY

HENRY *is on the witness stand.* JIMMY *and* PAULIE *are present in court.*

EDWARD MCDONALD: Mr Hill, this morning you told the members of this jury about your background, isn't that right?

HENRY: Yes.

EDWARD MCDONALD: You told them about your childhood growing up in the East New York section of Brooklyn?

HENRY: Yes.

EDWARD MCDONALD: You told them about your early life of criminal activity, including gambling, hi-jacking and loan-sharking?

HENRY: Yes.

EDWARD MCDONALD: Now did you come to know a man by the name of James Conway?

HENRY: Yes.

HENRY: (*Voice-over*) It was easy for all of us to disappear. My house was in my mother-in-law's name. My cars were registered to my wife. My social security cards and driver's licenses were phonies. I never voted. I never paid taxes. My birth certificate and my arrest sheet, that's all you'd ever have to know I was alive.

EDWARD MCDONALD: Do you see him here in this courtroom today?

HENRY: Yes.

EDWARD McDONALD: Will you please point him out for the members of the jury. (HENRY *points to where* JIMMY *is seated*.) Your Honor, please let the record reflect that Mr Hill has identified the defendant James Conway. Mr Hill, do you also know a man by the name of Paul Cicero?

HENRY: Yes.

EDWARD McDONALD: Do you see him here in the courtoom today?

HENRY: Yes.

EDWARD McDONALD: Can you point him out for the members of the jury? (HENRY *points to where* PAULIE *is seated*.) Your Honor, let the record reflect that Mr Hill has identified the defendant Paul Cicero. Your Honor, I have a document that I'd like to have marked for identification. I believe that it should be government exhibit twelve.

HENRY: (*Voice-over*) See, the hardest thing for me was leaving the life.

EDWARD McDONALD: May I approach and have it marked for identification? Thank you.
(*Later*.)

HAYES: Mr Hill, you became an informer to get out of jail, is that right?

HENRY: Yeah, I guess you could say that.

HAYES: And you've heard people refer to informants . . .

HENRY: (*Voice-over*) I still love the life. And we were treated like movie stars with muscle. We had it all, just for the asking. Our wives, mothers, kids, everybody rode along. I had paper bags filled with jewelry stashed in the kitchen. I had a sugar bowl full of coke next to the bed.

HAYES: . . . as rats, isn't that right?

HENRY: Some people use that word, yup.

HAYES: And people call 'em rats 'cause a rat will do anything to survive. Isn't that right, Mr Hill?

EDWARD McDONALD: Objection!

JUDGE: Objection sustained.

HENRY: Look, I don't know nothing about being a rat.

HAYES: Mr Hill, you know everything about being a rat!

EDWARD McDONALD: Objection, Your Honor! In view of the violence in Mr Conway's case, minimum sentence of twenty years' incarceration. In all the other circumstances here the

applicable guidelines require that you impose a minimum
sentence of twenty-five years' incarceration.

HENRY: (*Voice-over*) Anything I wanted was a phone call away.
Free cars. The keys to a dozen hideout flats all over the
city. I bet twenty, thirty grand over a weekend and then I'd
either blow the winnings in a week or go to the sharks to
pay back the bookies.

(HENRY *leaves the witness stand and speaks directly to the
camera.*)

HENRY: Didn't matter. It didn't mean anything. When I was
broke I would go out and rob some more. We ran
everything. We paid off cops. We paid off lawyers. We paid
off judges. Everybody had their hands out. Everything was
for the taking. And now it's all over.

EXT. A STREET IN A MIDWESTERN TOWN. DAY

*The camera tracks down the street until stopping at a house where a
man in a dressing gown opens his front door to pick up a newspaper.
It is* HENRY.

HENRY: (*Voice-over*) That's the hardest part. Today everything
is different. There's no action. I have to wait around like
everyone else. Can't even get decent food. Right after I got
here I ordered some spaghetti with marinara sauce and I got
egg noodles and ketchup. I'm an average nobody. I get to
live the rest of my life like a schnook.

In a final image, TOMMY *fires a gun at the camera, then the
following titles come up:*

Henry Hill is still in the Witness Protection Program. In 1987 he
was arrested in Seattle, Washington, for narcotics conspiracy
and he received 5 years' probation. Since 1987 he has been
clean.

In 1989 Henry and Karen Hill separated after twenty-five years
of marriage.

Paul Cicero died in 1988 in Fort Worth Federal Prison of
respiratory illness. He was 73.

Jimmy Conway is currently serving a 20-years-to-life sentence for murder in a New York State prison. He will not be eligible for parole until 2004 when he will be 78 years old.

Music Featured in GoodFellas

'Rags to Riches'
Written by Jerry Ross and Richard Adler
Performed by Tony Bennett

'Can't We Be Sweethearts'
Written by Morris Levy and Herbert Cox
Performed by The Cleftones

'Hearts of Stone'
Written by Eddie Ray and Rudy Jackson
Performed by Otis Williams and The Charms

'Sincerely'
Written by Harvey Fuqua and Alan Freed
Performed by The Moonglows

'Firenze Sogna'
Written by Cesarini
Performed by Giuseppe di Stefano

'Speedo'
Written by Esther Navarro
Performed by The Cadillacs

'Parlami d'Amore Mariu'
Written by Enrico Neri and C. A. Bixio
Performed by Giuseppe di Stefano

'Stardust'
Written by Hoagy Carmichael and Mitchell Parish
Performed by Billy Ward and His Dominoes

'This World We Love In' ('Il Cielo in una Stanza')
Written by Toang, Mogal and Raye
Performed by Mina

'Playboy'
Written by Brian Holland, Robert Bateman and
William Stevenson
Performed by The Marvellettes

'It's Not for Me to Say'
Music by Robert Allen
Lyrics by Al Stillman
Performed by Johnny Mathis

'I Will Follow Him' ('Chariot')
Written by Norman Gimbel, Arthur Altman, J. W. Stole and
Del Roma
Performed by Betty Curtis

'Then He Kissed Me '
Written by Phil Spector, Ellie Greenwich and Jeff Barry
Performed by The Crystals

'Look in My Eyes'
Written by Richard Barrett
Performed by The Chantels

'Roses are Red'
Written by Al Byron and Paul Evans
Produced by Bob Gaudio
Performed by Bobby Vinton

'Life is But a Dream'
Written by Raul Cita and Hy Weiss
Performed by The Harptones

'Leader of the Pack'
Written by George Morton, Jeff Barry and Ellie Greenwich
Performed by The Shangri-Las

'Toot, Toot, Tootsie Goodbye'
Written by Ernie Erdman, Ted Fiorito and Gus Kahn

'Happy Birthday to You'
Written by Mildred J. Hill and Patty S. Hill

'Ain't That a Kick in the Head'
Written by Sammy Cahn and Jimmy Van Heusen
Performed by Dean Martin

'He's Sure the Boy I Love'
Written by Barry Mann and Cynthia Weil
Performed by The Crystals

'Atlantis'
Written by Donovan Leitch
Performed by Donovan

'Pretend You Don't See Her'
Written by Steve Allen
Performed by Jerry Vale

'Remember (Walkin' in the Sand)'
Written by George Morton
Performed by The Shangri-Las

'Baby I Love You'
Written by Ronny Shannon
Performed by Aretha Franklin

'Beyond the Sea'
Written by Jack Lawrence and Charles Trenet
Performed by Bobby Darin

'The Boulevard of Broken Dreams'
Written by Al Dubin and Harry Warren
Performed by Tony Bennett

'Gimme Shelter'
Written by Mick Jagger and Keith Richards
Performed by The Rolling Stones

'Wives and Lovers'
Written by Burt Bacharach and Hal David
Performed by Jack Jones

'Monkey Man'
Written by Mick Jagger and Keith Richards
Performed by The Rolling Stones

'Frosty the Snow Man'
Written by Steven Nelson and Jack Rollins
Performed by The Ronettes

'Christmas (Baby Please Come Home)'
Written by Phil Spector, Ellie Greenwich and Jeff Barry
Performed by Darlene Love

'Bells of St Marys'
Written by Douglas Furber and Emmett Adams
Performed by The Drifters

'Unchained Melody'
Written by Hy Zaret and Alex North
Performed by Vito and The Salutations

'Danny Boy'
Written by Frederick E. Weatherly

'Sunshine of Your Love'
Written by Jack Bruce, Peter Brown and Eric Clapton
Performed by Cream

'Layla'
Written by Eric Clapton and Jim Gordon
Performed by Derek and The Dominos

'Jump into the Fire'
Written by Harry Nilsson
Performed by Harry Nilsson

'Memo from Turner'
Written by Mick Jagger and Keith Richards
Performed by The Rolling Stones

'The Magic Bus'
Written by Peter Townshend
Performed by The Who

'What is Life'
Written by George Harrison
Performed by George Harrison

'Mannish Boy'
Written by McKinley Morganfield, Mel London and Ellas
McDaniel
Performed by Muddy Waters

'My Way'
Written by Claude Francois, Jacques Revaux and Paul Anka
Produced by Steve Jones
Performed by Sid Vicious

Faber Film

Woody Allen
Pedro Almodóvar
Alan Bennett
John Boorman
Joel and Ethan Coen
David Cronenberg
Sergei Eisenstein
Peter Greenaway
Graham Greene
John Grierson
Trevor Griffiths
Christopher Hampton
David Hare
Hal Hartley
Derek Jarman
Neil Jordan
Krzysztof Kieślowski
Hanif Kureishi
Akira Kurosawa
Louis Malle
Harold Pinter
Dennis Potter
Michael Powell
Satyajit Ray
Paul Schrader
Martin Scorsese
Don Siegel
Steven Soderbergh
Preston Sturges
Tom Stoppard
Andrey Tarkovsky
Robert Towne
François Truffaut
Andrzej Wajda
Wim Wenders